PICCOLO BOOK OF
AMAZING SCIENTIFIC FACTS

PICCOLO BOOK OF AMAZING SCIENTIFIC FACTS

JANE SHERMAN

Cover illustration by Camm Ashbrook Associates Ltd
Text illustrations by Robin Lawrie

A Piccolo Book

PAN BOOKS LTD
LONDON

First published in Great Britain 1961 as *The Real Book of Amazing Scientific Facts* by Dobson Books Ltd
This abridged edition published 1974 by Pan Books Ltd, 33 Tothill Street, London SW1

ISBN 0 330 23875 2

*Made and printed in Great Britain by
Cox & Wyman Ltd, London, Reading and Fakenham*

For

Hilda, David, Peter, Erica, Vicky,
Nicky, Buffy, Debbie *and* Laura Jane

The author wishes to express her deep gratitude to Margaret Gossett and Franklin Watts for the many valuable suggestions they made during the preparation of this book, and to Ned Lehac, that most patient teacher of science, for his helpfulness and skill in criticizing the manuscript.

The author also thanks Dr G. H. H. Tate, curator, Department of Mammals, The American Museum of Natural History, New York City, for his kindness in reading the section on mammals for this book; Dr Peter van de Kamp, Sproul Observatory, Swarthmore College, Swarthmore, Pa, for reading the section on astronomy; and Alice Dickinson, author of *The First Book of Plants*, for reading the section on plants.

Contents

A Word about Facts

PERHAPS you have heard the story of the three blind men who were taken to 'see' an elephant for the first time in their lives. One man stood near the animal's trunk, touching it with his sensitive finger-tips. The second man stood by the elephant's side and ran his hands over its rough surface. The third man stood by the elephant's hind leg and put his arms round it to feel its shape.

When the elephant had been led away, each man was asked to describe the creature he had just 'seen'.

'That's easy,' said the first man. 'An elephant is very much like a snake.'

'Why, it is *not*!' protested the second man. 'An elephant is as high and flat and broad and wide as the side of a barn.'

'You're both wrong,' cried the third man. 'Anyone can tell that an elephant is built like a post, straight up and down and as big round as my two arms can reach.'

9

What each man had described from his limited experience was a fact. The elephant's trunk *is* like a thick snake, the side of its body *is* as big and flat as the side of a small building, and its legs *are* round like posts. But no one of these facts alone correctly describes the whole animal. Only if the facts were all put together and many other facts added could another blind person get a clear picture of an elephant.

That story illustrates an important fact about facts. No one fact by itself – nor even, sometimes, quite a few facts – is enough to give the whole truth about anything. You should remember, therefore, that the real facts in this book are like the appetizers that are often served before a big dinner. They are intended to excite your appetite, but they are not supposed to be the entire meal!

If these facts arouse your interest and curiosity in the sea, the earth, the sky or any other subject, then you will want to read some of the hundreds of books that have been written about each topic. In this way, you will go on from one single amazing fact to the even more amazing, more complete truth about a particular science or subject – at least, as far as is known today.

If you do this, you will not make the mistake of the blind man who thought the elephant's trunk was the whole animal!

1
Old Mother Ocean

THE sea may have been the original mother of us all. Present-day scientists believe that the ancestors of all life, from the tiniest one-celled structures to the largest animals, began in the sea.

Sunlight reaches only one-third of all the ocean water in the world. This means that more than half the total area of the earth is covered by water which is so many miles deep that no sunlight can penetrate its depths.

At one time a great part of Europe, Asia and North America was covered by sea. Indeed it is only a comparatively short time ago in geological terms (i.e. just a few million years) that these continents began to take their present-day form.

All living animals – whether fish, reptile, bird or

mammal – have a salty mixture running through their veins. This mixture is inherited from their ancestors who lived in the ocean. The chemical elements called sodium, potassium and calcium are found in animal blood today in almost exactly the same proportion as they are found in sea-water.

All life is thought to have come originally from the sea to the land, but there are some animals who went back to live in the sea. Fossils suggest that the ancestors of whales used to be mammals who lived on the land. They were probably enormous beasts of prey with large and powerful jaws and teeth. Millions of years ago, scientists think, they ate fish, crabs and other marine animals which they caught at the edges of the ocean and along the banks of river deltas. Perhaps over the years they began to follow their food out into deeper and deeper water. Slowly, their bodies adapted themselves to conditions in a watery world. Their front legs became flippers. (If the body of a whale is opened, the remains of his hind legs can be seen clearly near his tail.)

Gradually, the theory goes, such prehistoric beasts became so used to living in the sea that they began to spend all their time there. They developed into the whales, sea lions, seals, sea elephants and other sea mammals we know today.

The first living thing to move from the ocean and

try to live on dry land is believed to be a kind of sea-weed. Then, about 350,000,000 years ago, the first animal crawled from the sea and began to live at least part of the time, on the land. This was a sort of scorpion.

The seas are rising in most parts of the world. Measurements taken along the Atlantic Coast of America from Florida to Massachusetts between 1930 and 1948 showed that the ocean had advanced about four inches into the coastline during those eighteen years.

Many fantastic tales have been told about sunken islands. But here is a story about the actual discovery of such an island.

During the Ice Age, a million years ago, the waters of the North Sea, near what is now England, were drawn up into glaciers, exposing the bottom of what had been the sea. Since it was good rich land, trees and other land plants began to grow there. Animals came from the mainland to live in the fertile forests that developed. Early men hunted these animals with stone weapons.

When the glaciers began to recede, floods caused by the melting ice cut off the forests from the higher mainland and made an island in the sea. The primitive huntsmen on this island probably escaped in boats from it to the mainland. But most of the animals were caught, and when the water finally rose high enough to cover the entire island, they were drowned.

No one knew this sunken island existed until early this century, when some fishermen, trailing their nets in the North Sea, found large animal bones caught in them when they were hauled up from the deep water. They also discovered pieces of trees and stone instruments among the fish flopping in the nets. They took these unusual things to scientists, who recognized them to be plants, bones and weapons belonging to the Stone Age. From their knowledge that this part of the North Sea had once been land, the scientists were able to reconstruct the history of the lost island, which lies about sixty feet beneath the surface of the water and is almost as large as Denmark. It is called Dogger Bank and is a well-known fishing ground.

Sea anemones have such brilliant colours and flower-like shapes that they are called 'animal flowers'. They are really a kind of marine animal which often lives to be a hundred years old.

Islands in the South Pacific are constantly appearing or disappearing. Falcon Island rose very suddenly out of the sea during a sub-marine volcanic eruption in 1885. It was two miles long, and parts of it rose 250 feet above sea level. Then it began to slip back into the ocean. By 1895, only ten years after it was first discovered, Falcon Island had completely disappeared. It has reappeared and disappeared several times since.

Other South Pacific islands disappear more slowly, but also for no known reason. Ponynipete, in the Carolinas group, is such an island. Here a person can go out in a boat and see the waves breaking over the deserted homes in what was once a town. Ponynipete is gradually sinking back into the sea.

Baffin Island, an island the size of England, lies in the Arctic Ocean near Greenland. During the Ice Age, ice a mile in thickness covered the land. The tremendous weight of this mass of ice pressed the island 200 feet down into the sea. But now the ice-cap is melting. The weight of the ice is gradually becoming lighter, and the whole island is rising slowly out of the sea at the rate of six feet every hundred years.

The Persian Gulf contains the hottest ocean water in the world. It sometimes reaches 96 degrees Fahrenheit.

The Red Sea got its name from the millions and millions of tiny forms of sea life that live in it. Each body – individually the size of a tiny berry – is red, and together these colonies redden the water in which they drift.

The Red Sea has the saltiest ocean water. The hot sun that burns down on it most of the time causes rapid evaporation of the top layer of water. As this layer turns into vapour, its salt particles are left behind. These drop down into the next layers of water, making them very dense and salty indeed.

The saltiest water in the world is found not in an ocean, but in the Great Salt Lake, in Utah in the United States and in the Dead Sea. Their salinity is six times greater than any ocean's. No fish can live in such salty water. Any fish that may be carried into the Dead Sea by the River Jordan quickly die. The only animal life in the Great Salt Lake are tiny brine shrimps found along its edges.

Because it is so salty, the Salt Lake has never been known to freeze, even in the coldest winter. Only a few lumps of ice have been formed along the coast line.

The salt in salt water makes it heavier, or denser,

than fresh water. For this reason salt water is better able to hold up a body than fresh water. No one can sink in the Great Salt Lake because of its exceptional density.

The Dead Sea lies farther below sea level than any other body of water in the world. It is 1,300 feet below the level of its nearest sea neighbour, the Mediterranean. The water in the Dead Sea is warmer than the air above it.

Large rivers that flow into the sea often change the saltiness of the water near their mouths. Because the huge Amazon River of South America pours such an enormous amount of fresh water into the ocean, the sea water is sometimes fresh enough to drink as far as a hundred miles out in the ocean from the Amazon's mouth.

You may have heard the phrase 'the seven seas'. There are no special seven seas. This is an expression that has been used for centuries by many different peoples to mean many different bodies of water. In modern times, the seven seas are thought to mean the Arctic, the Antarctic, the North Pacific, the South Pacific, the North Atlantic, the South Atlantic and the Indian Ocean.

There is no ocean water that belongs *only* to the Atlantic, or *only* to the Pacific, or to any other ocean. The breakers you dive into or jump over at Blackpool may once have touched the sands of African beaches, or the rims of Arctic icebergs. Then they travelled to Lancashire along the deep, dark underwater roads of hidden currents. These hidden currents connect all the oceans of the world. They cover about three-quarters of the entire globe.

The single greatest explosion of all remembered time was the destruction of an island in the sea. Lying in the Sunda Straits between Java and Sumatra was an island named Krakatoa (pronounced crack-a-**toe**-a). On this island was a large, active volcano called Maha-Meru. On 27 August 1883, this volcano erupted with such violence that almost the entire island exploded. Although the island originally stood from 300 to 1,400 feet above the level of the sea, after two days of constant volcanic eruptions all that was left of it was one slim edge of the crater of Maha-Meru. Its bottom was a thousand feet *below* sea level.

A column of stones, dust, white-hot lava, steam, molten rocks, smoke, ashes and snow and ice shot up seventeen miles into the sky. The forests of nearby islands were buried under great drifts of dust and lava. The area of their land was increased by the addition of rocks and stones. In the town of Batavia in Java, one hundred miles away from Krakatoa, the sky was so darkened by clouds of

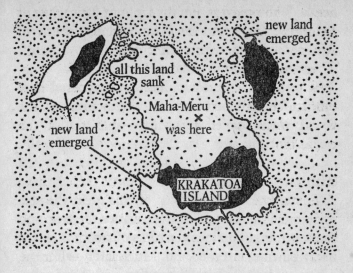

**AFTER THE GREAT EXPLOSION ON KRAKATOA
ONLY THIS PART WAS LEFT**

ashes that people had to keep lamps lighted during the two days that the eruption lasted.

On no other recorded occasion has sound been known to travel such a great distance. The thunder of the explosion was heard in Australia – *2,250 miles away*! It was also heard in Ceylon, 2,058 miles away, and in Bangkok, Siam, 1,413 miles away in a different direction.

The violent eruption caused an enormous tidal wave some hundred feet high. This wave swept first along the Sunda Straits, wiping out whole villages on the islands there, drowning more than 36,000 people, and sinking ships in the harbours. It travelled with great speed to the Indian Ocean, reached the southernmost tip of Africa, went round the Cape into the Atlantic and, thirty-two and a half hours later, it reached the English Channel – 11,040 miles away!

The clouds of volcanic dust and powdered rock that had been blown out of the very heart of the island were carried by winds right round the world. For the next year they caused exceptionally brilliant sunrises and sunsets in almost every country.

The only known survivor of this great disaster was a small monkey. A few days after the eruption she was found floating on a piece of wood. She was badly burned, but she lived. Much later – after the ashes and lava that covered it had cooled enough – scientists visited what was left of Krakatoa. Not a single living plant or animal could be found either under or on top of the layer of ashes and lava. Months after the eruption, one scientist did report finding a tiny spider. It was busy spinning its web!

'Tidal' waves have nothing to do with tides. Such waves are either sea waves, caused by undersea earthquakes, as at Krakatoa, or wind waves, caused by tremendous hurricane winds. The correct name of the sea waves is *tsunami* (tsoo-nah-mee), a Japanese word.

The worst known wind wave produced by hurricane winds occurred in 1737 in the Bay of Bengal,

India. It drowned some 300,000 people and sank over 20,000 boats.

The force in a large storm wave as it crashes against the shore is often powerful enough to smash huge breakwaters made of concrete. During a winter gale in Scotland, waves destroyed a concrete breakwater that weighed over 1,200 tons. A new pier was built in its place. This weighed 2,320 tons. That, too, was carried away by storm waves.

Tides rise and fall mainly in response to the pull of the moon (and a little to the pull of the sun) on the waters of the oceans. Along most coastlines of the earth the tide rises or falls only a few feet twice a day. But this is not true of the tides in the Bay of Fundy, which lies between Nova Scotia and New Brunswick, in Canada.

Because this bay is shaped like a funnel with a very narrow mouth, high tide waters rush through its small entrance all at once. This causes the water in the bay to rise often as much as seventy feet. These are the highest tides in the world. It is estimated that nearly 100,000,000,000 tons of water pour into the Bay of Fundy with a rising tide.

Fresh-water springs are often found in the ocean near coasts. They are usually made by underground streams that flow beneath the sea bottom, then break through its surface to empty into the sea itself. There is one such spring off the coast of Florida, near St Augustine. Because fresh water is lighter in weight than salt water, it rises to the surface there in such quantity that it makes a patch of bubbles which can be seen clearly.

This fresh water is often 'caught' and used in places where drinking water is hard to find on land. People who live on the Bahrein Islands in the Persian Gulf and on certain islands in the South Seas dive to the bottom of the sea near one of these springs and scoop up the fresh water in containers.

There is more in the sea than salt, seaweed and fish! Many valuable chemicals and minerals are to be found there. For instance, one cubic mile of water contains nearly 115,000,000 tons of common

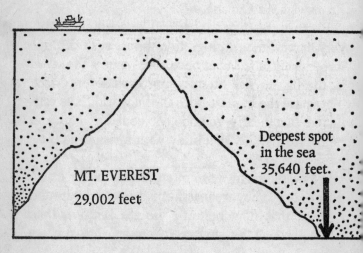

Deepest spot
in the sea
35,640 feet.

MT. EVEREST
29,002 feet

table salt; over 16,000,000 tons of magnesium chloride; 7,000,000 tons of magnesium sulphate (which we call Epsom salts); 5,268,000 tons of calcium sulphate and 320,000 tons of magnesium bromide. The same cubic mile also contains smaller quantities of iodine, iron, copper, silver and gold.

The deepest known spot in the sea anywhere in the world was discovered in 1951. It lies in a part of the Pacific Ocean known as the Marianas Trench, south-west of Guam. The depth is 35,640 feet – or more than *six and a half miles*! This goes deeper below the surface of the sea than Mount Everest, the highest mountain, rises above sea level.

Scientists who study the sea and its creatures can now use a specially designed underwater television camera. Instead of sending a man in a diver's outfit to the bottom of the ocean, they send a TV camera with lights to illuminate the floor of the sea. With a long-distance focusing device, the scientists then sit on a ship on the surface of the water and watch the TV screen!

Scientists can make imitation sea water by putting together the same chemicals that make up sea water in the same proportion as they are found in the ocean. But no forms of marine life will live in this man-made water. Yet if the scientists add just a small proportion of *real* sea water to their artificial sea water, marine plants and animals will flourish!

2
Rocks, Rills, Valleys and Hills

Our earth is about three thousand million years old. Some scientists believe it may be four thousand million years old.

The earth has a radius of about 4,000 miles from its centre to its outer crust. The deepest mine man has dug goes down two miles into this thick crust. This is only as deep, comparatively, as a day's accumulation of dust on a cricket ball.

At sea level the usual pressure of air on our bodies is 14·7 pounds per square inch. But the pressure on the centre, or core, of the earth is about 50,000,000 pounds per square inch. Experts are not yet agreed on whether this core is a solid, a liquid or a gas.

It is believed by many scientists that the inside of the earth is very hot. According to this theory, the heat escapes little by little. As the earth cools, it is contracting, or growing smaller, at the rate of a few inches every hundred years.

The rocks of which mountains are made are generally lighter in weight than the rocks of which plains are made. The very heaviest rocks of all are to be found under the bed of the ocean. If mountains were made of rocks that were as dense as these undersea rocks, the mountains would be so heavy they would sink back down into the centre of the earth.

A group of islands called St Paul Rocks are believed to be made of this dense material from the floor of the sea. They are a quarter of a mile long, and their highest peak is only sixty feet above sea level. They lie in the Atlantic Ocean between Brazil and Africa. For thousands of years, waves from thousands of miles of open sea have broken over these islands. The rocks still stand. But nothing grows on them, not even lichen – that tough, grey-green, scaly stuff which seems to grow under any conditions. The only 'inhabitants' of these desolate rocks are some crabs, some sea birds, and a few insects and spiders that live on the sea birds.

Sand makes up a large part of the earth's surface. The largest desert in the world is the Sahara in North Africa, which is 3,500,000 square miles in area, or larger than the United States. The depth of its sandy surface varies from a few inches to 300 or 400 feet, but not the whole desert is sand. It has many mountains and many spots called 'oases', where there is water and where plants can grow.

It also has many underground streams. In some places, when people dig through the sand to reach these underground rivers, they catch live fish in the fresh water.

Almost everyone thinks that quicksand is a special sort of sand with some mysterious power to suck a person or thing down into its depths. This is not true. Quicksand is merely the name given to sand which is unusually saturated, or filled with water. This makes the sand almost liquid, and so thick and sticky that a weight easily sinks down into it and is held fast.

Have you ever heard of 'singing sand'? This is a kind of sand that makes odd sounds when it is walked on or driven over, or when the wind blows across its surface. The sound such sand makes is something between a crunch and a squeak, but it often has a definite musical pitch.

People in different parts of the world have given these musical sands different names. In South Africa they are called 'crying sands'. In Hawaii they are called 'barking sands'. And in Afghanistan they are called 'drumming sands'. But whatever the sands may be called, scientists have not yet agreed as to what causes them to make such peculiar noises.

The nine highest mountain peaks in the world are all in the Himalayas, in or near India, Nepal, Pakistan and Tibet. No wonder this region is called 'The Roof of the World'!

The highest known waterfalls in the world were discovered only as recently as 1935. These are Angel Falls, in Venezuela. They are eighteen times higher than Niagara Falls, and more than twice as tall as the Empire State Building. They fall a total of 3,212 feet.

The Antarctic continent near the South Pole is a vast, snow-covered, almost totally unexplored area of the earth. It is about 5,000,000 square miles in size, or roughly as big as the United States and Australia together. But it has been visited by very few people. This is probably because it is the world's coldest land – far cooler than the lands nearest to the North Pole. Even at the sea-shore in the middle of summer, the temperature is freezing. In winter, the temperature is believed to drop as low as 100 degrees below zero.

Snow often falls so heavily in the Alps, the Rockies and other high mountains that its great weight and the force of gravity cause it to slide downhill. A huge snowslide is called an avalanche. As the original mass of snow rushes down it collects more snow. Like a gigantic snowball (although it is not round), an avalanche gathers both speed and size until it buries everything in its path.

Avalanches are most likely to come in the spring. At that time the warmer air and sunlight start to thaw the frost which may have held the snow-drifts in place. When the snow breaks loose from the mountain-top and slides some distance down a steep slope, it may reach a speed of 100 miles an hour. In the Swiss Alps, an avalanche has been known to contain 5,000,000 tons of snow. Such an enormous mass moving at such tremendous speed often creates a powerful wind. The wind made by an avalanche has blown down trees and houses half a mile away from the great snowslide itself.

There are delicate moments when a mass of snow is balanced between the force that wants to pull it down the mountain-side and the force that wants to hold it in place. At such moments of equilibrium, or balance, the smallest vibration may start an avalanche sliding – even the vibration of sound waves produced by a sudden noise. For this reason, guides in Switzerland may forbid mountain climbers and skiers to shout or talk loudly during the avalanche season.

The largest hailstone yet to be measured, weighed and photographed before it melted was one that fell in Nebraska in 1928. It was seventeen inches round and weighed one and a half pounds.

On the island of Dominica, in the British West Indies, there is a volcanic lake that boils constantly. This lake is hidden in the jungles on a mountain-side 2,300 feet above sea level. It is 300 feet wide, and 300 feet deep at its shores. But no one has ever measured its depth in the centre. The water is boiling hot. Sulphur and other chemicals in it raise its boiling-point temperature from the usual 212 degrees to 219 degrees Fahrenheit.

Like bubbles in boiling soup, bubbles made by underwater gases cover the surface of this lake. Sometimes they are thirty feet across, and sometimes one is so large that it covers almost the entire lake. The tops of these bubbles often swell up ten feet into the air before they burst. The gas released when the bubbles finally do burst is so poisonous that it has been known to kill explorers who smelled it.

The highest recorded temperature of lava that burst out of a volcano was 4,000 degrees Fahrenheit.

Volcanic steam has been used to supply power in three places in the world: Tuscany in Italy, in Java, and in California in the United States. The supply of this natural steam in all three places shows no signs of lessening or growing weaker in pressure. Wells similar to oil wells have been drilled into the ground where volcanic steam was known to exist. The steam is then used to generate electricity. Although this source of natural power has not been fully developed, scientists are still interested in its possibilities.

There is a dry lake bed in the Panamint Mountains near Death Valley, California, which has geologists puzzled. On this lake bed are huge boulders, some of which weigh as much as 500 pounds. Paths across the dry mud clearly show that these enormous stones move from one place to another. But there are no tracks of tyres, horses' hoofs or any other means of pulling these stones. What makes them move?

Scientists admit that they do not know. No human being is known actually to have seen the stones move. It is believed that the stones may skate over the dry earth when the lake bed tips back and forth. Or when the bed becomes slippery with rain and mud, strong winds may push the heavy stones as if they were sailing-boats. But until more is known about the forces that move these huge boulders, they will remain a scientific mystery.

3

The Universe in the Sky

PROBABLY the most amazing fact about the sky is its size. So get ready to read a lot of very, very big figures.

In our part of the universe (called a galaxy) there are millions and millions of stars. But our galaxy is only one of at least 100,000 other galaxies that are as big or even bigger than ours.

Astronomers measure the unbelievably enormous distances in space by what they call 'light-years'. Light travels at a speed of about 11,000,000 miles a minute, or nearly six billion miles a year. Astronomers say that our galaxy is 100,000 light-years wide. This is easier than saying it is six hundred thousand billion (600,000,000,000,000,000,000) miles wide, although both mean the same thing.

The light from the moon, 238,857 miles away from the earth, reaches our eyes in about one and one-third seconds. The light from the sun (93,000,000 miles away) reaches the earth in about eight minutes. Light from the fairly close star Sirius takes a little over eight years to reach the earth. But light from a star on the very outer rim of space in some distant galaxy travels some *thousand million* years before it reaches our earth! Because of this we may see its light long after it has 'died' and is no longer shining.

Stars look small because they are so far away. Actually, some of them are so large that their size cannot be imagined. Betelgeuse is about 260,000,000 miles across – about 30,000 times the diameter of our earth.

With thousands of stars of such enormous size in the sky, you might think space would be crowded. But it is not. This is how one astronomer explained it: 'If you let just three wasps fly in the air over Europe, that air would be more crowded with wasps than space is crowded with stars!'

Mankind has kept records of eclipses of the sun and the moon for nearly 4,000 years. The earliest record we have of an eclipse of the sun was made in the year 2283 BC, when there was a total eclipse over a Sumerian city called Ur, which was in the country now known as Iraq.

When we look up at the sky on a clear night, it seems to us that we see millions of stars. But we can see only one-half of the sky at a time (because the other half is on the underside of the earth), and astronomers have calculated that the largest number of stars that can be seen at one time by the naked eye is 3,000.

If you use a good pair of field-glasses, you can see about 120,000 stars. And if you could look through one of the large telescopes, you would see about 1,500,000,000 stars. But there are still many, many more that have not yet been seen.

The sun is nearly 400 times the size of the moon. But it is also 400 times farther away from the earth. That is why the sun and the moon appear to us to be about the same size.

The sun is about 3,000,000 miles nearer the earth in January than it is in July.

It was thought that the sun was a mass of molten iron and other heavy elements. It is now known that the sun is made up of about 81 per cent hydrogen and about 18 per cent helium, with only about 1 per cent of heavy elements. Since both hydrogen and helium are gases, the sun is for all practical purposes a fiery ball of gas.

The sun measures 865,000 miles across. The temperature at its centre is estimated to be nearly 29,000,000 degrees Fahrenheit.

The sun moves at a speed of about 650,000 miles an hour through our galaxy and draws the planets with it.

In three minutes the earth receives more energy (heat and light) from the sun than it receives from all the millions of tons of coal that are burned in the whole world during a year.

A man who weighs 165 pounds on earth would

weigh 4,620 pounds if he were on the sun. This is because the sun's force of gravity is twenty-eight times greater than that of the earth.

There is not just one moon in our solar system, but thirty-one, by the latest count. And astronomers think there may be even more!

The moon is the only heavenly body that has ever been known to move round the earth. It makes one complete trip every twenty-seven and a third days, or thirteen complete revolutions in one year.

Although the moon appears to shine, it has no light of its own. All its light is reflected from the sun.

You would think the full moon is twice as bright as the half-moon. But it is not. A full moon is *nine times* as bright as a half-moon. This is because we can only see that part of the half-moon which is very rough and hilly. There are so many shadows on the rough surface that it reflects very little light from the sun. When the moon becomes full there is a great deal more smooth surface to be seen, which reflects almost all the total amount of light.

Five planets can be seen at night with the naked eye, but they are not always visible at the same time. They are Venus, Jupiter, Saturn, Mercury and Mars. The other planets are too far away and too small to be seen without a telescope.

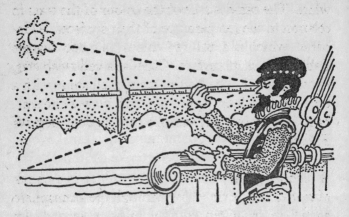

Polaris is the name of the North or Pole Star. It is one of the most important stars in the sky to us because the north pole of our earth points directly at it. As the earth turns, it looks as if the sky and all its bodies rotate round the Pole Star. Because this star stays in one place, it helped to guide sailors and explorers at night for hundreds of years before complicated instruments were invented. During the day they 'shot the sun' with their cross-staffs.

Through telescopes, astronomers have been able to see when the seasons change on the planet Mars. They note that during the winter each pole of Mars is covered with a white cap which is probably ice.

When iron is first heated, it turns a dull red; with greater heat, it turns bright red, then brilliant white. The same is true of the colour of the stars in relation to the temperature of their surfaces. Aldebaran, which is a dull red colour, is 6,000 degrees Fahrenheit at its surface. Capella, a yellowish star, is twice as hot. The hottest stars of all shine with a blue-white colour. Spica, a bright blue-white star, has a surface temperature of 36,000 degrees Fahrenheit!

A 'shooting star' is not a star at all. It is a chunk of matter that is travelling through the atmosphere anywhere from ten to fifty miles a second. Its correct name is a 'meteor' while it is flying through the sky. If it lands on the earth it is called a 'meteorite'.

These hard bodies move so fast that they become white-hot and finally either explode into flaming vapour or land on the earth. Those that have fallen on the earth and have been examined were found to be made of iron, nickel and a stone that resembles volcanic rocks. The meteors we see in the sky may have been flying through space for anything from two to two thousand million years.

The largest meteorite that can be seen is called the Hoba Iron. It is stuck in the ground near a place called Hoba West, in South-West Africa, and it weighs sixty tons. Another huge meteorite fell in

Siberia in 1908, leaving an enormous hole in the ground. It made such a powerful blast of wind when it landed that it blew down trees for miles around.

Diamonds have been found in meteorites.

Astronomers estimate that approximately 60,000,000,000 tons of meteorites have fallen on the earth in the last 60,000,000 years. The weight of the earth is increased by nearly 1,000 tons every year as a result of meteoric material, mostly dust, that falls from the sky and lands on the earth's surface.

Comets are quite different from meteors. Meteors shine because they are heated to a white-hot colour by friction caused by the tremendous speed of their passage through the atmosphere. Comets, however, fly millions of miles away from the earth's atmosphere. They shine with a bright light not because they are hot, but because sunlight is reflected from the myriads of dust particles that make up the comets.

A rainbow occurs when drops of rain, mist or spray split up light rays from the sun and reflect them. A prism of glass breaks up rays of white light in the same way, turning the white into a ribbon of its seven colours: red, orange, yellow, green, blue, indigo and violet. These colours are present in a rainbow, but the human eye usually cannot see or distinguish them all. A person looking at a rainbow usually sees only a band of red, a band of yellow, and a band of blue-green.

Did you know there were moonbows as well as rainbows? They are made the same way as rainbows, but use the light of the moon instead of light from the sun. Because moonlight is faint, moonbows are not often seen. The best condition under which to see one is after a shower at night, when the moon is bright and rather low on the horizon. Moonbows may also sometimes be seen in waterfalls at night.

Over the entire earth, meteorologists say, there are about 144,000 flashes of lightning every twenty-four hours. Lightning strikes somewhere on the earth about fifty times a second, or *over fifteen hundred million* times a year. Only one person in a million is killed by lightning, however.

Lightning breaks between clouds and strikes upward as often as it strikes downward. Only one bolt in a hundred hits the earth. Of course there is no truth in the old saying that 'lightning never strikes twice in the same place'. Lightning has struck the Empire State Building and other sky-scrapers many, many times – not only during different storms, but during the *same* storm.

4
Mammals on Land and Sea and in the Air

MAMMALS are animals which have warm blood and hair and whose females feed their young with milk from their own bodies. There are 3,500 different species of mammals. Of all these the animal called Man is the most amazing. He is the only animal that really talks, and the only animal that can learn from the experience of past generations and teach this wisdom to his children and grand-children.

Other animals are also unique in certain ways. The nine-banded armadillo, or peba, is the only mammal that always bears a litter of four babies of one sex at a time – always either all boy-pebas or all girl-pebas.

The only mammal whose eyes are of enormous size in proportion to the rest of his body is the tarsier. He looks like a little monkey, and he lives in Malaya, Borneo and the Philippines. Because he can see better with his remarkable eyes in the dark than in the light, he sleeps most of the day and he hunts his food at night. Without turning his body at all, he can turn his head completely round to look behind him.

The dog is man's oldest animal friend. The domestication of the dog was one of the most important aids in man's developing from a wanderer to a settler. This is the way it worked:

Men and women began to write down the records of their family and tribal history, build homes and create great works of art and science only after they no longer roamed over the land, hunting, killing and eating their food as they went. Only after they settled down to live in one place could they progress to become the human beings we know today.

But they could not settle down until they first learned to sow seed and gather and store plants to eat all the year round. And wild horses and cattle liked to eat the wheat, rice, rye and other food-crops men planted in their fields. So the earliest human societies could not have lived successfully in one place for any length of time until after wild dogs were trained to guard planted fields against hungry animals. This is why a famous historian has written that the taming of the dog is the most complete, the most unusual and the most useful conquest man has yet made.

Scientists remember with shame what greedy, thoughtless men did to the American buffalo. (His real name is *bison*.) Herds that totalled 50,000,000 bison used to roam the western plains. But by 1900 there were only about 800 bison left in the United States!

The Indians thought highly of this animal, as well they might. Dried and smoked buffalo meat gave them food. The buffalo's hairy hide was both bed and winter coat. The dressed skin made moccasins, leggings, shirts and women's dresses, as well as tepees, canoes and shields. Sinews provided thread for sewing, string for bows, and webs for snow-shoes. Braided rawhide or hair made ropes. Rib bones made runners for dog sleds. Hoofs yielded glue. The horns made cups and spoons, while small bones made needles. No other animal has been used by man for so many different purposes except the seal, which serves the Eskimo in many of the same ways.

Because the Indians could not kill too many bison with bows and arrows, the herds were fairly safe until the white man began to move westward. Then guns started the terrible killing. And greed for money from the sale of bison hides and meat nearly finished off the herds for good. The builders of railways slaughtered thousands to feed their gangs of workmen. Hunters used to ride on trains through enormous masses of buffalo, shooting the animals from the train windows. Often these 'sportsmen' would simply tear out the buffalo tongues to sell, leaving the bodies on the plains. The killing was so great and so senseless that the bison were almost wiped out.

Today small herds of American buffalo are carefully reared under government protection in national parks. There are now about 6,000 bison in the United States, and some 30,000 in Canada.

The largest member of the rodent family is an animal called a capybara (pronounced kap-ee-**bah** rah). He is four feet long, two feet high, weighs over 100 pounds, and looks like an enormous guinea pig. He lives near streams and rivers in South America. He has partly webbed feet to help him swim in and under water. He eats vegetables, especially sugar cane. But his teeth are said to be strong enough to chew right through corrugated iron.

Millions of years ago, the original horse (known to scientists as Eohippus, the Dawn Horse) was as

small as a little dog, and had five toes. Speed and silence were his only protection against large animals. He had the habit of running quietly on his toes. After thousands of years, his descendants gradually lost all but one of their toes on each foot. The horny nail on this toe became the hoof. So today's horses actually run on tiptoe.

Dipodomys is a desert animal who is nicknamed

'kangaroo rat'. His most important weapon of self-defence is his astonishing hearing ability. One half of his head is made up of resonance chambers that magnify every sound. He can even hear the vibrations made by a snake crawling into his under ground burrow. This Jerboa-like creature apparently never needs anything to drink.

If nothing happened to any of their descendants, one pair of ordinary rats could have more than 350,000,000 offspring in three years!

American pack rats sometimes enter a house to steal bright objects such as spectacles or coins. But they usually leave something in exchange, often an acorn. That is why Americans sometimes call them 'trader rats'.

One of nature's oddest and oldest mammals is the duck-billed platypus, the only mammal to lay eggs. The platypus is found only in Australia and Tasmania, where he lives in burrows along the banks of streams.

The platypus looks like a bad joke. He has a broad, flat bill like a duck's, webbed feet that help him to swim very fast, beady little eyes, long silky fur that resembles a mole's, and a flat tail like a beaver's. He grows to about twenty inches in length and weighs four pounds. Since he has no teeth, he eats worms, prawns, water insects, tadpoles, snails and other foods by crushing them between horny plates in his mouth.

The female platypus lays two eggs in a hole in a river-bank. For fourteen days she curls her body round them to keep them safe and warm. After they hatch she makes a sort of pouch by folding her large tail under her. There she keeps the hairless babies until their fur grows. The babies suck up milk which flows from large pores in the mother's body and runs through her fur.

When it comes to moving fast, the speed record for mammals looks like this:

Man can run about 25 miles per hour in short spurts.

A jack-rabbit can run between 35 and 40 miles per hour.

A racehorse runs between 45 and 50 miles per hour.

A gazelle can run at the rate of 60 miles an hour. A two-day-old baby gazelle can run faster than a full-grown fast horse.

And the swiftest of all mammals for short distances – the fastest animal to move on the ground – is the cheetah, a large member of the cat family which lives in Africa and southern Asia. He is often called the 'hunting leopard', because he is easily trained by man to hunt. He has almost the same affectionate nature as a dog. Within two seconds, a cheetah can get up a speed of 45 miles per hour from a standing start. And at the peak of his stride, he has been clocked at 70 miles per hour.

The smallest hoofed animal in the world is the mouse deer, which is found in Indonesia. He weighs five or six pounds, has a body about the size of a jack-rabbit's, legs only as large as pencils, tiny hoofs, and he stands only nine or ten inches high at the shoulder.

The very smallest mammal we know of is the pygmy shrew. This miniature mouse-like creature weighs less than a 2p piece and lives on insects and earthworms. Its head and body together are only one and a half inches long, and its tail is only about an inch long. It has a savage disposition, and this is probably how bad-tempered people got the nickname 'shrew', as Shakespeare used it in his play, *The Taming of the Shrew*.

The kangaroo has babies that are smaller at birth in proportion to the mother's size than the babies of any other mammal. Mother may stand nearly six feet tall and weigh almost two hundred pounds. She usually has one baby at a time. But baby is about an inch long and weighs well under an ounce.

A baby kangaroo is born blind, furless, and armed only with two strong little front feet that have claws. His hind legs are not as well formed as his front ones. He climbs up into the big, warm, fur-lined pouch which his mother wears over her stomach. There he immediately clutches a milk gland and starts swallowing. He is not strong enough to suck. But Mother has special muscles with which she pumps milk into him until he can eat by himself. He stays in the pouch for several months, until he weighs about ten pounds and has a good coat of fur. Then he starts hopping out once in a while to nibble the grass that will be his main food for the rest of his life. He hops back into Mother's pouch at any sign of danger. By the time he is a year old, he is usually on his own.

The camel is one of the most mysterious animal types in existence. Scientists think present-day camels are the descendants of prehistoric animals that were saved from extinction because men tamed and used them a long time ago. Camels today have many of the same physical characteristics they had millions of years ago.

In past ages the North American plains were covered with tiny camels about the size of sheep. For some unknown reason they all disappeared. Yet the camel is still primarily an American animal, for the llama, the alpaca, the guanaco and the vicuña of South America are all members of the camel family. The camels with which we are most familiar, though, are the one-humped dromedary and the two-humped camel of Asia.

The desert camel, known as the 'ship of the desert', is perfectly made for his hard life. He has sharp teeth which enable him to nip and chew roots and even thorns. He prefers to eat dry shrubs and wiry grasses. He drinks enough water to store about a gallon and a half – at least enough to last three or four days. This water is kept in 'tanks' that can be closed off from his stomach and opened when he wants a drink. His body tissues also function as storage cells. At the age of four months, he grows a lump of fat on his back. He draws nourishment from this fat when he has no other food to eat. This lump of stored fat is what makes the hump on a camel's back. His backbone does not bend upward at all.

In order to travel over the soft sand of the desert, he has broad, flat feet covered with rubbery skin. The flat feet act as 'snow-shoes' to carry him along, while their tough soles prevent his feet from being burned by the intense heat of the sand and also keep rocks from cutting them. Because he must kneel and lie on sand, as well as walk over it, he grows thick pads on the bottom of his belly and on his knees.

The camel has beautiful long eyelashes to keep his eyes clear of dust. And since he can open or close his nostrils as he wishes, he can breathe during a sandstorm without getting too much sand in his nose. Once he starts moving, he travels at a steady two and a half miles per hour, as regular as a machine.

Nature seems at first thought to have forgotten to provide the camel with any real weapon against his enemies, despite all his marvellous equipment. However, the storage-tanks in which he keeps gallons of liquid also produce an acid. When a camel becomes angry or annoyed, he spits a fine, strong spray of this acid liquid, which has a vile odour.

The sloth is an animal that spends most of his life

upside down. He hangs by strange, hooklike claws from tree branches. Because of these claws and the unusual length of his legs, he can walk on the ground only with difficulty. He moves slowly, as a rule, and so appears lazy (hence his name), although occasionally he can swing through the branches with considerable speed. During the rainy season in the tropical forests where he lives, a kind of green moss grows all over his long fur.

This weedy coat gives a faintly greenish tinge to the sloth's fur and makes it harder for his enemies to see him.

The giant ant-eater walks with his front claws bent backward under his feet. He has no teeth, but his mouth is big enough for a whip-like sticky tongue about a foot long. His claws rip open ants' nests, which are made of hard earth. He uses his tongue to sweep the ants out of their nests and up into his mouth.

The giant panda looks like a bear but is more closely related to the raccoon family. He is so rare that he has been known to scientists only in the last hundred years. He lives in bamboo forests in high mountains in China, and eats mainly bamboo shoots.

The opossum is the only animal in North America who has a pouch like the kangaroo's. Baby 'possums are so tiny when they are born that a whole litter of fifteen can be placed in a tablespoon. Although they may grow up to weigh fourteen pounds each, it takes about 40 new-born babies to equal the weight of one ten penny piece.

Skunks are usually not too eager to discharge the spray of foul-smelling fluid which is their weapon against enemies. They 'ration' it because their supply is limited. Once they have used it all up, they have no other real defence. The smell of skunk oil is so powerful that it can be recognized half a mile away if the wind is in the right direction.

As you probably know, bats are mammals with wings. Some are tiny, and some, like the flying foxes of Eastern Asia, have a wing-spread of five feet or more. But bats are *not* blind; they will *not* fly into your hair; and they do *not* suck blood.

Vampire bats that live in the tropics often do make a tiny cut in a large animal's skin while the animal is asleep. Their teeth are so sharp that they do not cause any pain when they pierce the skin. The vampire bat then laps up the blood that flows from the tiny cut. Such bats have a special substance in their saliva which prevents the blood from clotting. They do not suck the blood, nor do they drink enough to kill their victims. Many animals, including men, have been cut by bats while asleep and never known it.

The tallest of all animals is the giraffe. Sometimes he may grow to more than eighteen feet in height, and babies are often six feet tall when they are born. Giraffes look queer when they run because they move both legs on the same side of their body at the same time. But they can gallop as fast as thirty miles an hour with this funny, lop-sided gait.

A giraffe has hardly any voice and he seldom needs water. His markings make him almost invisible when he stands still among trees in sunlight and shadow, even though he is a large animal. His long neck enables him to eat leaves from the tops of trees on the African plains where he lives. But in spite of the length of his neck, a giraffe cannot just lower his head to reach the earth. In order to nibble grass or sip water from a stream, he must first

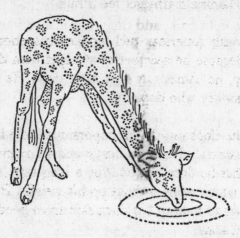

spread his long front legs wide apart. One last amazing fact about the giraffe: his eyes stick out so far from the sides of his skull that he can see behind him without having to turn his head.

Monkeys are as common in the New World as they are in Asia and Africa. In fact the monkeys of Latin America are the only kinds in the world that use their tails as 'fifth hands' with which to cling to branches.

A small South American monkey called the marmoset has the distinction of being the only kind of mammal in which the male takes almost complete care of his child. Until the little marmoset grows old enough to climb by himself, Papa marmoset carries him round on his back constantly, except when Mamma marmoset feeds him.

The South American owl monkey has enormous eyes. Because he sees better at night than during the day, he comes out only after dark. He is the only monkey who does this.

After the elephant, the hippopotamus is the largest land mammal. He is so heavy and so awkwardly built that he does not live for a long time out of water, which helps to hold up his weight. He also needs water to keep his thick skin from becoming dry and scaly.

It used to be thought that the hippo 'sweated blood' when out of the water. Now we know that what really happens is that a special reddish, oily perspiration comes out of pores in his two-inch-thick skin. This liquid protects his hide from the drying effects of the air for a short time. When he is excited, hot or hurt, the red fluid flows faster and is redder in colour. But this fluid is not blood.

The otter lives part of the time on land, part in the water, catching most of his food in rivers, streams and lakes. But if left alone, baby otters pay no attention to water and run around playing and eating entirely on land. Mother otter has to teach her young how to swim, dive, catch fish and stick their heads into muddy river bottoms to look for eels.

The bear family inhabits many parts of the Northern Hemisphere, and its largest member is the brown bear of Alaska. This bear can weigh as much as 1,800 pounds. Another American bear, the grizzly, is considered the most ferocious and most dangerous American mammal. The polar bear spends as much time in the cold Arctic water as he does on the Arctic ice floes. In spite of his huge weight – often 1,500 pounds – he prowls over this slippery ice with assurance. This is because the soles of his big flat feet are covered with fur which stops him from slipping.

Except for pouched animals like the kangaroo and opossum, a mother bear has the smallest babies for her size of any mammal. A bear cub is usually about nine inches long and weighs twelve ounces when born, although his mother may weigh 500 pounds.

Perhaps the most lovable looking of all animals are the original 'Teddy Bears', whose name is koala (pronounced koe-**ah**-la). They live in Australia. They are not really bears at all, but pouched animals.

In addition to looking sweet enough to kiss, with their shoe-button eyes, big toy-like ears, and woolly bodies, koalas are fearless and very intelligent. They were once numerous in their native land, but now they are so rare that the Australian Government is protecting them in much the same way that the American Government protects the bison.

It is difficult to keep koalas in a zoo because of their strange diet. They will only eat leaves from certain kinds of eucalyptus trees. And they insist on different species of leaves every other day or so, and if these are not offered they refuse to eat and starve to death. They grow to be about two feet tall, and Mother koala often carries her baby on her back as she climbs round the tree-tops where they spend most of their lives.

Moles have unusual fur which grows in such a way that it can be brushed forward or backward. This enables the mole to move back and forth easily in his narrow burrow.

The golden hamster of Syria lives in a dry, rocky country where food is very scarce. He has to store up large quantities whenever he finds it. To do this, he has huge cheek pouches that reach from his mouth right back to his shoulders.

Not the lion, but the elephant is the real lord of the jungle – the largest living mammal that walks the earth. A male African elephant can be eleven feet high and weigh up to 14,000 pounds, or over six tons. His ears may be three and a half feet long and two and a half feet broad, while his ivory tusks may be eleven feet long, eighteen inches round, and weigh over 250 pounds together. A new-born elephant baby stands three feet high and weighs 200 pounds.

The elephant's trunk is perhaps the most re-markable organ possessed by any animal. It can be twisted in any direction and is equally powerful in all positions. It has no bone, but its sinew and muscles are so tough that the sharpest knife can barely cut them. Yet this large, strong, clumsy-looking organ can pick up one tender blade of grass. It can also uproot a heavy tree and toss it round the elephant's head! The trunk is also the elephant's nose, and provides him with an extraordinarily acute sense of smell.

Although an elephant can lie down easily if he likes, apparently he hardly ever wants to do so. Thousands of African elephants have been seen asleep standing up, and seldom have hunters found any markings on the ground to indicate that they have lain down.

Elephants have such tough whiskers and thick skins that their keepers in the circus often 'shave' them with a blow-lamp!

Remarkable as his physical characteristics are, the elephant's intelligence is the most amazing thing about him. Scientists consider him the most intelligent animal next to the dog that man has ever trained for his own use. Although the elephant has long been a beast of burden in India and the Far East, it cannot be said that he is truly domesticated, for he will seldom breed in captivity.

When elephants are wild, they live in herds. Every member of a herd is loyal to every other member. When the herd is attacked, the strongest ones will make a circle round the babies, the sick and the old. And they will try to pick a wounded comrade up and carry him along to safety.

But an angry elephant is said to be the most dangerous of all living creatures. An elephant seems to have no sense of fear whatsoever when he is aroused. In Burma a wild elephant once saw a locomotive coming down the tracks through 'his' jungle. He probably thought this strange, noisy beast had no right to chug and puff through his territory. So the elephant charged directly down the track towards the oncoming engine. He met it head-on and was killed at once. Although the locomotive weighed nearly fifty tons, the enraged animal smashed in the front end and derailed it.

Elephants can also act with amazing self-control and discipline. A wonderful example of this occurred during a circus fire not so long ago. The elephants were tied up in tents which went up in flames. The animals were badly burned and they were in terrible pain. But when their keeper ran to save them, shouting an order, each elephant pulled up his stake with his trunk and then grabbed another elephant's tail. As they had been taught to do for a performance, they all marched out of the fire in perfect formation.

The largest animal ever known to have existed lives in the sea. This is a species of rorqual called the blue whale. (Whales are mammals, not fish, as you probably know.) The blue whale reaches 110 feet in length and weighs up to 110 tons.

Rorquals, or fin-back whales, are the most common whales in the seas today. They spend their summers swimming in the Southern Ocean. In spite of their enormous size, they cannot bite or swallow large food whole. Their entire diet consists of a sort of sea-soup made up of tiny living shrimp-like organisms called plankton. The whale snaps up about a ton of water in one mouthful. This water is strained through fringes of whalebone that line the whale's jaw. Then it pours out of his mouth, leaving behind all the solid matter it contained.

Fascinating whale facts would fill a book, but here are a few. In spite of their enormous size, whales are usually the most peaceable creatures in the sea. A whale baby is the biggest at birth of any animal baby on earth. He is often half as long as his mother, and much larger than a full-grown elephant. He grows very fast, adding weight at the rate of two to three hundred pounds a day. Whales travel all over the world's oceans. One whale was harpooned in the Pacific Ocean, but managed to escape. He was finally caught, the original harpoon still stuck in his body, in the North Atlantic. Whales also swim from the surface of the water down to depths of at least 3,200 feet. And whales have brains that are at least as well developed as the brains of horses or dogs.

The story of the mermaid – half fish, half woman – probably began when someone first saw a creature called a manatee. This is a large mammal which lives in tropical rivers and in the sea. It looks slightly like a seal but is somewhat fatter and slower moving. A mother manatee will often rear straight up out of the water, holding a baby manatee at her breast with one flipper. From a distance, she probably looks like a human mother holding a human baby, but possessing a fish's tail – a mermaid.

5

The Vegetable World

THERE are about two hundred thousand known kinds of flowering plants in the world.

A green leaf is one of the most common of growing things. Yet scientists have not been able to copy the green substance called chlorophyll (pronounced **klor**-oh-fil) and use it as a plant does to make food.

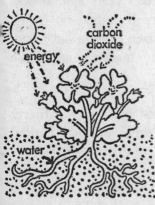

By means of chlorophyll leaves are able to capture sunlight's energy and use it to turn carbon dioxide from the air, and water from the soil, into glucose. This process is called 'photosynthesis'.

From glucose, by adding

minerals from the soil, plants make all the other materials they need for growth.

Most trees will 'drown', as people do, if they are planted in water so that their roots cannot get air from the soil.

The water that plants take in, but do not need – excess water – is given off by their leaves in vapour so fine that it cannot be seen. Every leaf constantly sprays out this vapour through its tiny pores. On a hot summer day a large oak tree gives off about fifty barrels of water in this way.

Scientists recently discovered a 'dawn redwood' tree alive and growing in China. Only its fossilized leaves had been seen before in rocks that were millions of years old. They were the remains of huge trees called 'metasequoias' which had lived from 30,000,000 to 60,000,000 years ago. It was thought this species of tree had died out some 20,000,000 years ago. But tree experts have now found a whole forest of living metasequoias in the middle of China.

The giant sequoia trees that grow in the Sierra Nevada mountains of the West Coast of the United States are probably the oldest living things in the whole world. Some sequoias are 3,000 years old. Many grow to be almost 300 feet high, or almost as tall as a twenty-storey building. They may measure 100 feet round at their base. The trunk of the largest known sequoia is estimated to weigh 1,000 tons. But the seeds of these giant trees are so tiny that 7,000 of them weigh only an ounce!

The sequoias that grow in California are carefully protected in government parks. Many people think the groves of these ancient, enormous trees make up one of the greatest wonders of the world.

It is said that sequoias never die of old age or disease. Their principal enemy is lightning.

Natives of the Indonesian islands call a certain kind of tree the 'silk cotton' tree. It has long pods similar to those found on milkweed plants. These pods are filled with silky fibres which are springy and have walls that do not absorb water easily. When used as stuffing they do not mat together. This buoyancy makes the silky stuff very valuable for life-preservers, boat cushions and life-jackets. You probably know its name: kapok.

A very old species of tree found in Africa is especially useful to the people who live there. This is the baobab (bay-oh-bab) tree. Although it does not grow very tall, its trunk may measure thirty feet across. Its wood is too soft to be of much use, but the Africans eat the gourd-like fruit and also make a drink from it. They burn the fruit pulp to make smoke that keeps annoying insects at a distance. A medicine is made from the bark, which is also used to tan leather. Bark fibres make rope, cloth, curtains and strings for musical instruments. Necklaces are made from the seeds. Dug-out canoes are

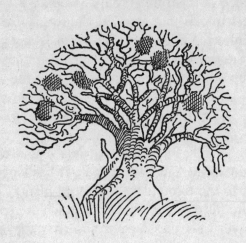

carved from the tree-trunks, or sometimes large decayed trunks are hollowed out by the natives and used as houses.

The banyan trees of India and Indonesia are the widest-spreading of all trees. As the branches of this tree grow, they drop roots down into the earth. As these roots become larger and tougher and covered with bark, they in turn become other trunks which grow more branches which drop down more roots, and so on. One banyan tree may have as many as a thousand trunks and cover a huge area of ground. One single banyan tree in India is said to have sheltered 7,000 people at one time – the army of Alexander the Great.

The palm tree is probably the tree that has been most useful to the greatest number of people in the world. From this one kind of tree, people who live in the tropics make:

coconut palm sugar	buckets
wine	baskets
vinegar	fences
fans	thatching for roofs
bedding and floor mats	musical instruments
sails for boats	food from seeds and
coconut oil	fruits
utensils from coconuts	fibres for clothing,
	hats and textile uses

And long before the invention of paper, medicine-men, poets and historians of the East Indian islands scratched letters on the fresh leaves of palm trees. They used a sharp bit of wood as a pen, then bound the palm fronds together to make books.

Dates from the date palm are one of the oldest foods known to man. Roasted date-stones are also often ground and cooked as a substitute for coffee.

North and South America gave the world many important food plants which it never knew before

Columbus made his voyage to the New World. Some of these are maize, tomatoes, potatoes, pineapples, tapioca, pumpkins, peanuts and chocolate.

The banana is one of the most important fruits of tropical countries. It is also one of the oldest of all fruits known to man, and one of the first to have been cultivated. It is mentioned in Chinese writings that are 3,000 years old.

Although banana stalks are called 'trees' and often grow thirty feet high, they are really huge herbs. Each stalk dies after bearing fruit, and a new one grows from an underground stem the next season. The seeds in cultivated bananas have dwindled until they are only black specks, incapable of growing new plants. New banana stalks are raised from cuttings or sprouts.

Bananas for marketing must be picked green and ripened later. If they are permitted to ripen on the stalks, they burst open, allowing insects to crawl in and spoil them.

Truffles are mushroom-like fungi which usually grow round the bases of oak trees. Because of their delicious flavour they have been nicknamed the 'diamonds of the kitchen'. They are small and black, and because of their rarity sometimes cost as much as forty pounds a pound. Because they grow from two to twelve inches below the ground, they are difficult to find. Trained dogs and pigs are used in France and Italy to find truffles. They sniff the earth round the trees. When they show that they have found some truffles buried there, they are rewarded with a bit of meat or a handful of meal by the truffle-hunter, who digs up the precious discovery with a blunt metal stick, packs the truffles in a basket and takes them to market.

The orchid is one of the most glamorous of all flowers. Orchids grow wild from the equator to the Arctic Circle and make up one of the largest flower families. Growing orchids from seeds is a slow and difficult process. Some seeds take from three months to two years to begin to develop as plants, and some will not grow at all unless a certain fungus that seems to be their partner is in the soil with them. The first blossom sometimes does not appear for seven or eight years. This is why orchids are so expensive. And especially rare kinds of orchids are very expensive. One single pure-white orchid plant discovered in the jungles of Colombia was sold to an orchid-grower in the United States for 10,000 dollars.

Some species of orchid imitate the appearance of different animals. They have the shape and colour of bees, butterflies, frogs, flies, lizards and even spiders.

An Indonesian member of the arum family has the largest flower in the world. This blossom pushes up a cylindrical shoot which grows longer rapidly and at the end of a few weeks is as tall as a man. Then a petal-like spathe unfolds around this. The whole flower may eventually reach a height of fifteen feet.

The next largest flower in the world is the *Rafflesia arnoldi*, which grows in Indonesia. Its blossoms measure three feet across the centre and weigh fifteen pounds. They have five petals, each of which may be one foot long and one inch thick. Rafflesias are parasites which live on the roots of other plants, and they have a very disagreeable odour.

There is a giant water-lily in Brazil which has leaves that are six feet in diameter. These enormous leaves, if protected by padding, will act as rafts, carrying people weighing as much as 150 pounds.

Since the earliest days of history, men have used plants for medicine. Some plants are still used in this way:

Cinchona bark gives us quinine to reduce fever.
Foxglove gives us digitalis to stimulate the heart.
Deadly nightshade gives us atropine to relax muscles.
Buckwheat gives us rutin, a drug to stop bleeding.
Seaweed gives us agar-agar, used as a laxative.

Coca gives us cocaine, which is used as a local anaesthetic.

As some animals eat plants, so do some plants eat animals. One of these animal-eating plants is the pitcher plant. This plant has leaves that form pitcher-shaped cups. Water collects in the cups and mixes there with a sweet substance which insects seem to love. When they climb into the cup to sip the sweet stuff, they often fall into the water and drown. The juices of their bodies are then absorbed by the pitcher plant. In Borneo their is *there* a huge pitcher plant with a cup nearly a foot wide, which can hold about a gallon of water.

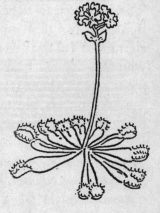

The venus fly-trap is a small flowering plant. Each leaf ends in two spiked halves which can snap together very fast, closing tightly around any insect that crawls over them. Then digestive juices from the leaf help the plant to absorb the insect as food.

The sundew is a short, low plant that spreads its reddish, circular leaves flat on the ground. These leaves are covered with long hairs which in turn are covered with a sticky glue. When an insect crawls or flies too close, it is caught by the glue. Then the hairs close all around it to keep it from escaping while the plant absorbs the insect with the help of acid juices.

The bladderwort eats very tiny water animals and insects. This plant grows under water and is equipped with air-filled sacs or bladders, which give the bladderwort its name. On the edge of each bladder a valve with an elastic opening leads inward. When tiny water animals swim or crawl through this valve it shuts at once behind them. There they are trapped and slowly absorbed by the plant.

The rubber tree is native to South America, although it has been transplanted to other tropical countries. Rubber was used by New World Indians who had learned to collect from certain trees the white sap-like latex from which it is made. Columbus, during his second visit to the New World, found Indians bouncing rubber balls. He took some of these balls back to Queen Isabella as a great curiosity. When this substance was first marketed, much later, it was sold only for rubbing out pencil marks. That is how it received its name: rubber. None of the innumerable uses rubber has today were discovered until centuries later.

The blossom of the night-blooming cereus has one

of the shortest lives of any flower known. The cereus is a kind of cactus found in Mexico. It blooms for only one night each year.

There are tiny red plants which grow in such great numbers on glaciers in the Arctic that explorers call them 'red snow'.

A beautiful silvery blue-green plant called silver-sword is one of the rarest plants in the world. It grows only inside a certain volcanic crater on the island of Maui in the Hawaiian Islands.

Hawaii has many plants that are found only on its islands and nowhere else in the world. One kind of violet was so specialized that when first found it grew only within an area of a few yards. And only one living specimen has been found of a certain tree.

In Indonesia there is a stinging nettle called *Laportea*. It looks like a small tree. It has green leaves with purple ribs and poisonous hairs. These hairs sting so badly when they are touched that the pain can be felt for a month afterwards. It is thought that if a man falls into such a tree he might die from its poisonous sting.

Growing in Latin America is the cow tree. Natives of Guatemala like the white juices of this tree because they taste very much like cows' milk and can be used as a substitute for real milk in sweet desserts.

A special Philippine coconut called 'makapuno' is filled with soft, jelly-like white meat. Ice-cream makers in the Philippines use this soft stuff to flavour a delicious ice cream.

A flower that grows high in the mountains of Switzerland forces its way through layers of solid ice to blossom in the sunshine. Its name is *Soldanella*, or ice flower.

The wild coffee tree was first known in Abyssinia,

in about 800 AD. It was probably first cultivated in southern Arabia, where, during its early history, coffee was sometimes prohibited as an intoxicating beverage.

The Mineral Realm
6

THE greatest storehouse of minerals in the world – largely unused – is the world's oceans. There are nearly 150,000,000 tons of dissolved mineral salts in one cubic mile of sea water.

Most table salt is mined from the earth, but some salt evaporates from the top of the sea and collects on shore. The Sambhar Salt Lake in northern India is an inland lake which acquires about 3,000 tons of salt a year in this way. The salt is blown there by hot, dry summer winds from the ocean – 400 miles away.

Magnesium is a light, strong metal used in making aeroplanes and many other products. It is found in the ground and also in the sea. In one cubic mile of ocean water there are about 3,500,000 tons of magnesium. Enormous quantities of ocean water can now be collected and treated with chemicals in order to 'mine' this valuable metal from the sea as well as from the earth.

Gold and uranium are each twenty times as heavy as water. Sodium and potassium are so light that they float on water, while lithium, the lightest of all metals, weighs only one-half as much as water.

Tin is one of the metals discovered, mined and used by man in early days. It was known to many ancient peoples, and it is mentioned several times in the Old Testament.

When tin and lead are melted, mixed, then cooled, they harden into something called solder. This is easily melted and is used as a kind of metal glue to join other metals together. Although made of tin, which has a melting point of 449 degrees Fahrenheit, and lead, which melts at 620 degrees Fahrenheit, solder's melting point averages only 360 degrees Fahrenheit.

Gallium is an odd metal which melts at 86 degrees Fahrenheit, that is, it would melt if you simply held it in your hand. But it will not come to the boil until it reaches a temperature of about 3,000 degrees Fahrenheit.

Glass is usually made by melting sand (silica), soda and lime together. Silica is one of the most plentiful minerals on the earth, so glass has long been used for many purposes. The Egyptians knew how to make glass before they built the pyramids.

Asbestos is a mineral which looks like spun glass. It has long, silky fibres that can be woven into a fabric. Its name comes from a Greek word which means 'unquenchable', and it has long been used where a fireproof material is needed.

Aluminium is the most abundant metal in the world. It forms about 8 per cent of the earth's crust. For a time after it was first isolated in 1812 it was more valuable than gold. Among the first articles of aluminium were a set of knives, forks and spoons which a French jeweller made for Napoleon III.

Mineral oils and petrol come from a substance called petroleum. Petroleum is believed to have been created when millions and millions of bodies of plants and animals, over millions of years, were buried beneath the surface of what used to be seas. The great oilfields of Oklahoma, for example, were formed in sediment and rocks under the seas that covered that part of North America in prehistoric times.

Coal began to be formed millions of years ago, when the huge trees and giant ferns of the jungles sank down into the deep mud of swamps. Geologists think that half the coal in the world – or over four billion (4,000,000,000,000) tons of this most valuable substance – is buried beneath the soil of the United States.

It would take a whole book to describe in detail the more than 200,000 different products that chemists can now make from coal. Here is a list of just a few things that are made either entirely of coal or contain a coal by-product: dyes, nylon, vitamins, sulphonamides, cooking flavours, aspirin, novocaine, the fluid in hydraulic brakes, telephones, unbreakable glass, anti-freeze solutions, synthetic rubber, DDT, benzene, mothballs and scent. (It takes over 2,000 pounds of real violets to make an ounce of violet oil – the 'essential' oil needed to make violet perfume. But for less than fifty pence a chemist can produce sixteen ounces of imitation violet oil from coal tar!)

The silver thread that marks temperature on the glass tube of a thermometer is the liquid metal mercury. Often called quicksilver, mercury is a unique metallic element. It is heavier than lead, it will freeze only at the low temperature of 38 degrees below zero Fahrenheit. Although it is a liquid, it will not make an object wet. It can be used to measure heat accurately because it always expands and contracts the same amount at a given temperature. Even if it should freeze, mercury will not

break the glass tube that holds it because, unlike water, it contracts instead of expanding when it freezes.

Sometimes the mercury in your thermometer may separate, one part staying at the top of the tube, the other near the bottom. When this happens, try one of the following tricks to pull it together again. Tap the thermometer, bulb down, in the palm of your hand. If that fails to work, tie a string round the tube and swing it like a lasso round your head. If this does not cause the two parts of mercury to join, put the thermometer in the freezing compartment of your refrigerator for a while. Unless the thermometer is broken, the cold will draw the liquid metal together again at the bottom of the tube.

Tungsten will not melt until it is heated to the incredible temperature of 6,098 degrees Fahrenheit. This is why it is often called the most 'stubborn' of all the metals.

Sulphur is a beautiful yellow mineral that gives off the horrible odour of rotten eggs when it is set on fire. Its nickname, brimstone, really means 'burnstone', for sulphur will burn if it is set alight. The sulphur in eggs will discolour a silver teaspoon. Sulphur is used to give us paper from wood pulp, matches, dyes, insecticides and medicines.

Hydrogen and oxygen combined with sulphur make sulphuric acid. This is called 'the king of chemicals' because it has such a very large number of uses chemically. Sulphuric acid helps to produce fertilizers for our farm crops, petrol for cars and planes, lubricating oils, rayon, cotton, wool or linen clothes, fire extinguishers, enamelled pots and pans, tinware, explosives, paints, plastics, leather, soap, fats, glycerine and food products.

After careful study involving microscopic observation over a period of years, scientists have discovered that there are tiny quantities of many different metals in human hair. These include potassium, sodium, magnesium, calcium, zinc, copper and iron.

Gold is one of the most remarkable of all metals because of the many unusual things that can be done with it. A kind of gold sponge is used to fill teeth. Gold is so easily shaped, or malleable, that one single grain can be beaten into a thin sheet almost eight inches square and four-millionths of an inch thick. It is almost impossible to imagine anything so thin. (A grain is an ancient measure of weight which is still used. Originally it equalled the weight of one seed, or one grain of wheat. The carat, which is used to measure precious metals and gems, gets its name from the bean that the Greeks used to measure gold, the carob bean. A carat equals approximately three grains in weight.)

Nearly half the world's annual production of gold comes from the mines in South Africa that often go down a mile and a half into the earth. The air at such great depths is cruelly hot and humid for the poor miners. They have to dig out tons and tons of worthless rock to get at the valuable gold.

But there is sufficient gold in all the waters of all the oceans to make every person in the world a millionaire – if it could be taken out of the sea cheaply enough. It is estimated that there is £33,000,000 worth of gold in one cubic mile of sea-water. But for just one part of the process necessary to extract this amount of gold from the ocean 200 tanks would have to be built. Each tank would have to be 500 feet square and five feet deep. Twice a day for every day of a whole year, men would have to fill and empty every one of these tanks. This operation alone would cost too much to make the process worthwhile.

Mexico and the United States are the leading countries in the world in the mining of silver. The Real del Monte mine in Mexico has been worked since the days of the Aztecs. It still produces five per cent of all the silver in the world.

Diamonds and all other gems belong to the mineral realm. The greatest diamond ever found was discovered in South Africa in 1905. It weighed 3,106 carats, or close to a pound and a half, and it was called the Cullinan. From this single rough diamond were cut nine large stones and several smaller gems.

The greatest diamond in the world is part of our own Crown Jewels. It is the Star of Africa, weighing 516½ carats, more than four times the weight of any other diamond. It was introduced into the king's royal sceptre by Edward VII.

It requires great skill and exceptionally steady nerves to cut a rough diamond into many brilliant gems. An expert often spends more than a year simply studying the stone, then tracing on it the lines where the cuts should be made that will give the finished diamonds their greatest brilliance. And the first cut into the rough diamond is the most important one. If it should crack the stone at the wrong angle, a diamond worth thousands of pounds may be almost completely ruined.

When the cutter came to make the first slice in the famous Vargas diamond, which had cost its owner a fortune, he was sick with nervousness. He lifted his hand holding a wooden mallet. He held in his other hand the steel wedge that would make the cut. He placed the wedge over the lines marked on the stone, which was firmly held in hard wax mounted on a wooden peg. Taking a deep breath, he finally hit the wedge with the mallet. When he saw that the split in the stone was perfect, the cutter fainted dead away!

Far more important than supplying jewellery is the valuable work diamonds do in industry. A diamond is the hardest of all known minerals. For this reason it is used commercially to cut other hard substances. It is the only gem that is made entirely of one element – carbon. Since it belongs to the coal family, a diamond will burn if it is heated to a high enough temperature. In spite of its tremendous hardness and durability, a diamond can be burned by a blow lamp.

A black diamond is a mass of impure diamond which is also called carbonado. It is not used as a gem, but is invaluable to industries that need tough drills, abrasive wheels, or sharp saws to cut through granite and marble. The largest black diamond ever found weighed 3,078 carats. It was discovered in Africa and sold as a curiosity for only a few thousand pounds. Although valueless as a gem, that same diamond would be worth several million pounds today if it were cut up and sold for industrial purposes.

Diamonds are often found on top of the ground as well as deep below its surface. Chickens eat stones to grind up the food in their crops, and ostriches in Africa have been known to swallow small rough diamonds for the same reason. People sometimes hunt ostriches and cut them open to see if they have swallowed any diamonds. One such 'living diamond mine' had more than fifty diamonds in his crop.

There is another jewel that is even more highly prized by some people than diamonds. This is emerald jade. Often called 'the royal stone', it is found mostly in the streams and quarries of northern Burma and Turkestan, then taken to China to be carved or polished. Jade is extremely hard and has magnificent shades of colour with delicate patterns in its grain. In order to carve it into figures, ear-rings, bowls or vases, a worker spends days drawing a taut wire backward and forward across the face of the rough stone. Then he works a foot-pedal lathe to shape the stone into a work of art. As no two fingerprints are alike, so it is said that no two pieces of jade have the same markings in their grain.

From gems to games is a big step. But marbles, too, belong to the mineral family, since they are made of glass that is made from silica. And they are useful in more ways than you might guess. Marbles are now made so perfectly that they can be substituted for steel ball bearings in certain machines. Engravers and lithographers use marbles to smooth the surface of their printing plates. Road signs are sometimes made of marbles with reflectors behind them to catch the light from car headlights. Acid-proof marbles are used by paper mills in paper-feeding machines. Ten glass marbles, melted at the high temperature of 2,500 degrees Fahrenheit, can be made into a square yard of the softest material. This glass cloth is fireproof, mildew-proof and waterproof. And marbles are even used by fish hatcheries. Placed on the bottoms of pools, they are supposed to look like eggs. It is said that their presence encourages the fish to lay more eggs during the spawning season.

Insects and Fish

7

INSECTS and fish are two of the oldest kinds of animal. (Yes, an insect is a member of the animal kingdom.) Insects are also the most numerous kinds of animal in the world – nearly 1,000,000 different sorts are already known to exist. Scientists believe many more are still to be discovered.

Scientists estimate that on or above every square mile of earth there are approximately 2,000,000,000 insects. To get an idea of how many there are, suppose you had a gigantic pair of scales. If you placed all the humans and large animals in the world on one side of the scales, and all the insects on the other, the side holding the *insects* would weigh more than the side holding all the humans and big animals!

It is said that every part of every plant, as well as every form of vegetable and animal matter, living or dead, is used as food by one kind of insect or another.

Locusts and some kinds of grasshoppers often travel in huge swarms, devouring all crops that happen to be in their path. In 1889 such a swarm flew in a black cloud over the Red Sea. This single swarm covered 2,000 square miles.

Most grasshoppers are vegetarians, but certain species eat animals. A four-inch-long African grasshopper is preserved in the British Museum (Natural History). Clutched in its front legs is a two-and-a-half-inch mouse which it had caught to eat.

Large water beetles often eat small, young fish. Giant water insects eat tiny frogs and tadpoles. Although spiders are not insects, according to scientists, because they have eight legs instead of six and two body sections instead of three, they are called insects by most people. Large South American spiders eat small birds, bats, snakes, lizards and fish. Enormous centipedes (for similar reasons not strictly considered members of the insect family) eat lizards and mice.

Certain insects can eat their way through metal. Beetles and termites have been known to chew through the lead covering of telephone cables. Tin, zinc and the quicksilver behind mirrors have also been chewed up by insects.

Insects are fantastically strong for their size. Beetles, for instance, have been observed to lift and carry bits of food weighing 850 times as much as they do. This is as if a man weighing twelve stone were to carry a load that weighed nearly sixty-four tons.

Although he has no wings and cannot fly, the average flea can jump 200 times his own length. If a man could jump the same distance in proportion to his size, he would be able to jump over the Great Pyramid of Cheops, Salisbury Cathedral, or even the Washington Monument!

Most insects either hibernate through the winter months or die. But a certain kind of daddy-long-legs, called the winter crane fly, spends his youth as an egg and then a larva hiding under decaying leaves during the summer. He becomes fully grown in the winter. From January to April, even when the temperature is below zero, he can be seen walking on his skinny legs over the snow. He is so sensitive to heat that he will die if carried just for a few minutes in a person's hand.

Many insects, like the familiar firefly, have their own lighting systems. One tropical American beetle has a small globe on each side of his throat. When he wants to see where he is going, the beetle can turn on these 'headlights'. When he is disturbed or scared, he keeps his lamps on for as long as five minutes at a time.

Since electricity is very rare in the jungle, South American natives often make use of these beetles. They put them in a wicker cage which they hang up in their house. When they want to 'turn on the light', they simply tap the cage. This so frightens the beetles that they all light up at once.

Men also use these special, luminous beetles to make a sort of torch. A short length of hollow sugar cane is cut in half lengthways. Several beetles are put in one half, which is then covered with a piece of netting. The other

half is closed over this. In the West Indies a gourd is used for this purpose.

When a man walking at night through a forest wants to see his path, he opens the sugar-cane torch, tapping or shaking the half which holds the beetles. They actually shine with a beam that is bright enough to help him find his way home.

Scientists exploring South and Central America often keep two or three light-making beetles in a bottle in their huts. They found long ago that they could read at night by the light the beetles make.

One kind of bumble-bee has a tongue long enough to pollinate red clover so that that valuable plant will bear fertile seeds. This fact led Charles Darwin to say: 'A lot of old maids living in a certain part of the country guarantees that red clover will grow there.' The great scientist explained his un-scientific sounding statement in the following way.

Bumble-bees are absolutely essential to the fertilization of red clover. Field mice attack bumble-bees. Cats attack field mice. Unmarried women (jokingly called 'old maids') often keep cats for companionship. Therefore, where there are women who keep cats, there are cats who catch field mice. The mice do not attack the bumble-bees, and the bees go about their business of fertilizing the red clover!

The buzzing or humming you hear from a bee is

not made by its throat but by its wings, which vibrate so fast – about 15,000 times a minute – that they make this noise.

Honey-bees use their tremendous wing speed to cool their hives. In the summer, special bees stand near the entrance to the hive and 'fly' without moving their bodies. This motion of their wings air-conditions the whole hive.

Science has produced many amazing chemical synthetics, such as rayon, nylon, saccharin and margarine. But science has not yet been able to make a successful copy of either the honey produced by honey-bees or the shellac made by lac insects.

Man is usually regarded as the only animal that uses tools but in fact there are are two insects that do so: a species of digger wasp and a species of ant.

A certain kind of female wasp digs a hole in the earth in which she lays her eggs. She then stuffs this hole with caterpillars for her babies to eat after they hatch. When the hole is full of food, the wasp looks for a tiny stone of just the right size. Holding it firmly in her jaws, she uses this pebble to pat down the earth over her precious nest, much as a man flattens a piece of soil with a hoe.

The tool used by some ants is a 'living sewing machine'. These ants make nests of leaves which are placed with their edges touching. To make these edges stick together, they use a seam of gluelike thread. Adult ants cannot manufacture this natural glue but baby ants make a thread from which they later spin their cocoons. So some ants hold the leaves in place, while others pick up baby ants in their jaws and hold them against the leaf seams. When they squeeze the babies' bodies, sticky threads of silk are forced from their mouths. The ants pass their babies from side to side across the leaves until the gluey thread 'stitches' their edges into a strong nest.

Ants are used by humans to sew up another kind of seam in another way. Indian doctors in South America, barbers in Smyrna and vets in Bali all know that certain giant ants continue to bite with a tremendous grip even after their heads are cut off. Our surgeons have thread or adhesive to close up a wound or incision. A South American Indian doctor may cleverly use ants. In his left hand he presses the edges of a wound together, and in his right hand holds a large ant in a pair of tweezers. Forcing its mouth open, he brings the ant close to the wound, and it bites down on both edges of the cut. The doctor then snips off the ant's body. Like a strong 'stitch', the ant's head continues to bite the edges of the wound together until it heals.

The smallest spider is only one twenty-fifth of an

inch long. The largest has a hairy body that is over three inches long, and a leg spread of more than eight inches. He lives in South America.

No known species of spider has wings or can fly. Like the flying foxes and flying snakes, the 'flying spider' of Australia has only 'parachute sails' with which it can float some distance through the air, from a higher to a lower altitude.

The fragile-looking thread spun by a spider is in reality the strongest fibre for its size of any fibre found in nature. A Brazilian spider spins a web made of thread that is even stronger than that most spiders make. Large as a good-sized wheel, this web hangs between trees. Its main body is suspended from the branches by four or five exceedingly tough silk threads. If an explorer in the jungle happens to walk into these threads, they will cut into his flesh as deeply as if they were thin wires.

Because spider silk is so strong and soft, many attempts have been made to find commercial uses for it. Two hundred years ago in France, gloves and stockings were actually woven from spider threads. But the only industrial use of this miraculous fibre today is in certain optical instruments.

Some spiders' webs in Australia measure nearly six feet across and are made of silk that is almost as thick as darning wool. Australian aborigines use these enormous, tough webs for fishing. This is what they do. They set up long bamboo poles, with a loop at their ends, near the place where they have found these big webs. The spiders soon make new webs on the loops of the poles, and these become perfect fishing nets. The web is so strong that neither the weight of the water nor that of a small fish will tear it. The fisherman stands by the side of a stream, pole in hand. When he sees a fish, he scoops it up in his spider-web net.

Human bodies are built to stand an average pressure of 14·7 pounds per square inch of air. Marine animals that live at a depth of 3,000 feet in the sea are built to stand a pressure of about 1,350 pounds per square inch of water on their bodies.

No sunlight or moonlight penetrates the deepest waters of the oceans. But some kinds of deep-sea fish make their own lights. The male uses his lanterns to help him find his female at the mating season, or to show her where he is. His lamps throw a strong beam of light through the black waters, and he can flash them on or off.

Fish belong to the group of animals called vertebrates, which are animals having a jointed spine. The smallest fish in the world is also the smallest vertebrate in the world. This tiny creature lives in the Philippines. He is about the size of an ant – less than half an inch long. His name is *Pandaka pygmea*.

And a trigger fish found in water near Hawaii has a name that is longer than he is – humuhumunuku-nukuapuaa!

Some species of fish live at great extremes of temperature. Desert minnows found in hot springs in

western America seem quite at home in water as warm as 125 degrees Fahrenheit.

In Alaska and Siberia, on the other hand, small fresh-water blackfish have been known to remain alive when frozen solid in a cake of ice. They were kept outdoors in baskets for weeks until needed for food. When brought into the house and thawed out, the fish came back to life. While still frozen, some of them were fed whole to dogs. They thawed out in the warmth of the dogs' stomachs and began to move around. This tickling so upset the dogs that they vomited the fish, still alive and wriggling.

Extraordinary in looks, the sea-horse is also extraordinary as a father. He has a pouch somewhat similar to a kangaroo's. When mating, the female drops from 200 to 600 eggs into this pouch. For approximately forty-five days Father Sea-horse carries these eggs around with him. Then one tiny baby – about the size of a comma – is born. And finally all the hundreds of eggs hatch into little sea 'colts'. Their bodies are transparent and do not acquire colour until the babies grow older.

Survivors of a type of fish that lived three hundred million years ago are the lung-fishes of South America, Africa and Australia. They reach a length of from one to six feet long, look like eels, and have gills like other fish. But they also have lungs, breathe air, and make a cry like a cat. They are a sort of 'missing link' between sea animals and land animals. When the water in their pond dries up, they dig into the mud, roll up in a tight ball, and go to sleep until the rainy season, breathing through a small tube in the mud. They may live in this way for several years.

Mudcakes containing lung-fish have been dug up and sent to museums. The lung-fish could be lifted out of the mud to be examined without waking up. But when placed in water they woke up at once.

Fossil bones show that back in the Coal Age, millions of years ago, there lived a kind of fish called a coelacanth (pronounced see-la-kanth). No living specimen of this animal had ever been caught in recorded history, and it was believed that this type of fish had been extinct for 75,000,000 years. But in 1938 fishermen trawling off the coast of South Africa were startled to find a strange-looking monster in their net. Light blue-green, about five feet long, it weighed 127 pounds and had a large head and strangely shaped fins and tail. It was a coelacanth.

By the time scientists got to it, most of the soft parts of its body were gone. They posted descriptions of it, and offered a reward for the capture of any new specimen. Luck was with them, for late in 1952 a slightly different species of coelacanth was caught – again off the coast of Africa. This new 'living fossil' has been preserved in good condition, and is being carefully studied. One scientist has said that the discovery of the coelacanth is 'perhaps the most amazing event in the realm of natural history in the twentieth century'.

One kind of angler fish lives in very deep, dark water. Hanging over the female's mouth is a long, flexible filament like a fishing rod. (It is in fact a modified dorsal fin.) The end of this rod can light up. If a small fish swims close to examine this lighted bait, the angler lowers it into her large mouth. The little fish follows the light, the angler pulls the bait out of the way, shuts her mouth, and eats the little fish.

The male of this species is very small. He attaches himself to the large female rather as a flea sticks to a dog. Like a flea, he gets all his nourishment from her body. And when it is mating time, the female does not have to swim all round the black water in search of the male. He is always with her.

If the angler fish can be called a 'fishing fish', the archer fish can be called a 'shooting fish'. This small marksman lives in the waters of the East Indies and eats insects. But he prefers flying insects to other kinds, so he 'shoots' them down. He takes a large mouthful of water. As he waits near the surface of his pond or river, he sees a small fly sitting on an overhanging tree branch. He sticks his head up and forces the water out of his mouth in a fine spray that hits the fly as accurately as if he had aimed with a water pistol. The spray knocks the fly down into the water, where the archer fish promptly eats it. He has been known to hit an insect that was six feet above the water.

Some fish can generate electricity – electric catfish of Africa, electric rays of tropical seas, and electric eels of South America. Electric eels (which are not eels at all, but related to carps and catfish) have two special glands extending from the back of the head through the long tail. These glands can discharge enough electricity to knock a man down. The electric eel uses his shock machine to knock out the fish he wants to eat, or to defend himself. This electric discharge is said to show the fastest rate of conduction known in living tissue. It flashes from the tail to the head of the eel at a speed of half a mile a second, or even more.

At the New York World's Fair in 1939 there was an electric eel on display which provided enough current to operate a radio, run a miniature train and light a series of 300 neon bulbs.

Fish move in other ways than by swimming. Some kinds fly, jump, crawl, and even climb. The gurnard, a marine species found in Europe, America and Indonesia, has three projections like fingers which stick out in front of his fins. Using these alternately, he can crawl in a clumsy fashion. The climbing perch can crawl as high as seven feet up a wet tree at the edge of his pool.

A small fish with a big name – periophthalmus – lives in the tropics. He hops around on mud-flats looking for his food, and has been seen on the roots of mangrove trees near the water. In addition to being able to move over land, he has adjustable vision. His large eyes can see in the air as well as in water. He has special muscles with which he moves the lenses as we adjust binoculars.

Moving at a speed of twenty to thirty miles per hour, a flying fish can cover several hundred yards

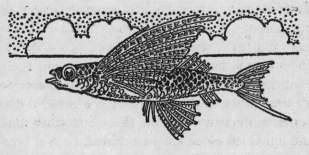

in the air. He is actually a glider with power, rather than a flier, however. He swims rapidly just beneath the surface of the water, until he is moving fast enough to 'take off'. When he enters the air, he holds out his side fins stiffly like wings. This enables him to soar quite a distance before descending into the water again.

The very fiercest fish we know of is not a shark, but a small South American creature called a piranha (pronounced peer-**an**-ya). This 'man-eater of the fish world' lives in the waters of the Amazon and Orinoco rivers. From six inches to a foot and a half long, he has a red belly and tail, silvery back and golden head. He looks as harmless as a fat goldfish but he is afraid of neither man nor beast. Cattle wading across a stream have been attacked by schools of these fearless, razor-toothed fish. A person who carelessly lets a hand trail in the water beside his boat may have the flesh of a finger neatly nipped off by a passing piranha. Scientists claim that a human being has a better chance of escaping from a school of sharks than he has of staying alive if he falls among a school of piranhas.

The gouramis have a pleasanter way of using their mouths than for biting or killing. Certain species of these little tropical fish kiss each other. No one knows quite why they do this. But when one gourami is left alone before a mirror, he will even kiss his own reflection.

Reptiles and Birds

REPTILES – animals that crawl close to the surface of the earth – are believed to be the ancestors of birds, animals that fly high above the surface of the earth. All birds and most reptiles lay eggs. And all birds still wear reptile scales on their legs.

A reptile is an animal that moves on its belly or on very short legs. The members of this family include snakes, lizards, turtles and crocodiles. The largest of these are the crocodilians – alligators and crocodiles.

The Egyptian crocodile with the unpleasant nickname 'man-eater of the Nile' kills more human beings a year than any other wild animal in all Africa.

A reptile holds the world's record for long life. One Galápagos tortoise has a recorded age of 200 years.

Most animals stop growing when they reach maturity. But turtles and certain other reptiles keep growing bigger as long as they live.

Some South Sea tortoises grow to weigh over 600 pounds. Specimens of leather-backed marine turtles have weighed nearly a ton and were eight feet long.

Snakes are among the most numerous and most fascinating of the reptiles. Contrary to most people's ideas, snakes are not slimy. Their skin feels like the bark of a dry, smooth tree, and they are among the cleanest of all animals.

A snake never winks or closes his eyes. He even sleeps with them open. This is because he has no eyelids, only an immovable transparent membrane, like a window, fixed over each eye to keep out dirt and dust.

Different kinds of snakes catch their food in different ways. But all snakes swallow their food whole. And many snakes eat eggs or animals which are larger than they are.

The largest and most active of all the poisonous snakes in the world is the king cobra. He is built like a whip and grows from fifteen to eighteen feet long. His body is a pale olive colour; his head is often orange with bright staring bronze-coloured eyes. He lives in India, Burma, Malaya, and Southern China. Many scientists consider him the most deadly of all living creatures.

The king cobra is thought to be very intelligent. When he is alarmed, he gives a deep hiss that sounds something like a muffled sneeze. His neck slowly expands into a long, narrow 'hood'. He can hold himself upright on the coil of his body to the height of a man's chest. His strike is not very fast. He sweeps forward to bite, and if you see him coming, there is time to jump out of his way before he strikes.

Rattlesnakes are called the 'gentlemen among snakes' because they usually warn before striking. Scientists believe, however, that this is nothing but a nervous habit over which a rattlesnake has no control. When excited and ready to strike, he moves his tail. This causes the rings of dry, hard skin at its end to rattle. Certain other kinds of snakes which have no rattles vibrate their tails in the same way when excited or frightened.

There are some countries where no snakes are found unless they have been brought in from other lands. These are mostly islands, such as Ireland, Hawaii, Iceland, the Azores and New Zealand, which have no native snakes. There are very few snakes in this country too.

The so-called 'glass snake' is a kind of lizard. If he is grabbed by his long tail, it breaks off to allow him to escape. No blood shows where the tail breaks away from his body, and after a while, a new tail (sometimes two!) grows to take the place of the old one.

Desert lizards, nicknamed 'sand fish', wriggle through fine sand as if they were swimming in water.

The basilisk of Central and South America is one of the few lizards that will have anything to do with water. Normally about two and a half feet long, he has a slender tail and legs, with especially big feet that have very long toes. When startled, he jumps off a floating log into the water. Standing upright on his big feet, he runs over the top of the water to another log. He can stay on the surface of the water for a quarter of a mile if he runs very fast.

The horned toad is really a lizard. When alarmed, some horned toads shoot a jet of blood from their eyes for a distance of several feet.

The biggest lizard in the world is the Komodo 'dragon' – so called because he looks like a pre-historic dinosaur, or drawings of dragons made by ancient peoples. He is a giant monitor lizard who lives on the island of Komodo, in Indonesia. From ten to thirteen feet long and weighing up to 250 pounds, he rules the island. He is very quick and active for his size, as well as being very strong and savage. He eats wild pigs with his huge teeth, and he is powerful enough to kill a horse if he had to. He has been seen to take the whole hindquarters of a deer in his mouth at one bite – legs, hams, hoofs and backbone.

The only known poisonous lizard is the Gila monster of the American south-west and Mexico. The Gila monster bites and hangs on to his victim like a bulldog while poison oozes from glands in his jaws. He has a large tail in which he can store up food. When he has lots to eat, his tail is big and fat. When he cannot find anything to eat, he lives on the nourishment he has stored up in his tail. The tail then becomes thin.

The lizard with which many people are probably most familiar is the chameleon. Everyone knows that he is famous for his ability to change the colour of his skin to match the colour on which he may be standing. But not everyone knows all the other amazing things he can do.

For instance, he does not always change his colour simply to protect himself by matching his background. He also changes colours with his feelings, as human beings blush red when embarrassed, or grow pale when frightened. The chameleon has a remarkable tail. He uses it as a sort of fifth hand, as a monkey does. The chameleon's tongue has been called 'the most amazing tongue in nature'. Exceedingly long and worm-like, it flicks out like a flash of lightning to catch an insect on its sticky end. A seven-inch-long chameleon can 'shoot' a fly that is twelve inches away from its nose – in less than half a second.

But perhaps the most unusual physical feature of a chameleon is his eyes. They stick out from his head on 'turrets' which revolve in sockets. Each eye can move in a different direction from the other. Thus while looking at the ground for possible enemies with his left eye, the chameleon can, at the same time, look overhead with his right eye for possible insects to eat. Or while peering ahead with one eye, he can also be staring behind him with the other!

Of all the different kinds of birds, the hoatzin (pronounced ho-**at**-sin) of South America most closely resembles his early ancestors. He is a living fossil who still clearly shows signs of having been a lizard many millions of years ago.

Like the extinct lizard-bird of those times, the hoatzin has a thumb and forefinger near the tip of each wing. These remnants of what must once have been feet have sharp claws. While the bird is a baby – before his wings develop and he learns to fly – he can climb trees by using his feet and these wing-fingers.

The largest bird ever known to science is the moa. Now extinct, the moa once lived in New Zealand. It sometimes grew to be over twelve feet tall and had legs longer than a horse's. The largest bird living today is the ostrich of Arabia and Africa; it may be eight feet high and weigh 300 pounds. The bird with the biggest wing-span is the albatross that flies over the southern oceans. His wings may spread as wide as fourteen feet from tip to tip, although his body may weigh only eighteen pounds.

The smallest birds in the world are the humming-birds, which live only in the Western Hemisphere. One species measures only two and three-eighths inches from the tip of his beak to the end of his tail. Their bodies, without including bill or tail, are only one and a half inches long. His size is not the only remarkable thing about a humming-bird, however. There is hardly a flying trick he cannot perform. With wings beating so fast you can hardly see them, he can hover in one spot like a tiny, brilliant helicopter. He can fly forward at almost sixty miles an hour, and can also do a very rare thing for a bird: he can fly backward.

The hummer's legs are so thin that they cannot support his very light weight. He seldom walks on the ground. But in his small body beats the largest heart in proportion to his size of any bird in the world. His strong heart and his unusually powerful wing muscles are what enable the little hummer to fly more than 500 miles every spring – from Central America to various parts of the United States – and back again, when cold weather comes! They also give him the strength and courage to attack birds many times his size.

But the thing people notice first and love best about the hummer is his magnificent colouring. In bright sunshine he looks like a flying jewel. This is why some of the different kinds of humming-birds (there are over 500) have names like ruby, emerald, and topaz. This is also why cloaks made entirely of humming-bird skins were worn by Aztec princes. And some American Indians sometimes wore humming-bird bodies as earrings.

Hummers seem to be the bravest of all wild birds. They will fly close to your face without fear. And in Central America they often go right into a house to build their little nests behind pictures or on door-ledges.

Certain birds are among the fastest-moving creatures known. A swift can fly as fast as seventy miles an hour. (A swift is so perfectly streamlined that his nostrils are made pointing backward instead of forward.) A golden eagle can fly at the rate of 120 miles per hour, while some hawks reach the great speed of 165 miles per hour.

Sight is a bird's most important sense. It is said than an eagle can see a mouse from a thousand feet up in the air. A large vulture, so high in the sky that a human cannot see him, will swoop down on to a dead rabbit which he has spotted from the air.

Baby birds belonging to a certain Australian species have a small 'light' in each corner of their mouths. These luminous organs show their mother where to put the worms and caterpillars she has brought back to the dark nest.

The pigeon is the only bird known to drink by sucking water up into its mouth and swallowing it. All other birds have to throw their heads back to swallow after each sip.

Most birds have a very weak sense of smell. But the kiwi (pronounced kee-wee) of New Zealand finds the insects and earthworms he eats by sniffing for them through nostrils at the end of his long bill. Often called the queerest and most un-birdlike of birds, the kiwi is very rare. He is covered with greyish-brown feathers that look like hair, and he has no visible wings. He sleeps all day and hunts at night. Near his bill he has long, threadlike feathers similar to a cat's whiskers. These help him to find his way about.

Human greed, which almost destroyed the American bison, did wipe out what was once the most numerous bird in the United States – and perhaps in the world. The passenger pigeon was unlucky because he was both good to eat and easy to capture. About 1850, flocks three miles long and a mile wide were common sights. They blotted out the sun as they flew overhead. In one single flock of pigeons there were more than 2,000,000,000 birds.

But their great numbers could not save them from greedy hunters. In only three years, as many as 999,000 *dozens* of passenger pigeons were shipped from Michigan to New York butchers' shops. Boys were paid a penny apiece for each bird they caught or shot. Within sixty years the enormous flocks of passenger pigeons were gone.

Martha, the very last passenger pigeon of all the original millions and millions, died of old age in the Cincinnati Zoological Gardens in 1914. Ornithologists everywhere mourned this senseless extinction of a harmless species of bird.

The ivory-billed woodpecker is probably the rarest bird in North America. Some scientists think he may be the rarest bird in the whole world. He lives in the southern United States and eats insects which bore into dead trees. When the forests were cut down in the South the ivory-billed woodpecker began to die out. For a long time his kind was believed to be extinct. Then a few ivory-billed woodpeckers were seen in a swampy forest in Florida. The state set aside a 1,300-acre sanctuary for these few birds in the hope that they would live and breed there. In 1950 another pair of these rare birds was seen, so perhaps the species will not become extinct as has the poor passenger pigeon. It is believed that there are now no more than half a dozen ivory-billed woodpeckers in the sanctuary – and thus in the entire world.

The fulmar, a member of the petrel family, uses a jet of thick, bad-smelling oil to protect himself. If attacked, he squirts the oil from his beak. His body is so full of oil that Scottish islanders sometimes kill a fulmar, run a wick through his body, and burn it as a torch.

In spite of the fact that ducks spend a great deal of their time swimming in water, their bodies do not get wet. They are so well protected by oil and their feathers are so close together that their bodies actually stay dry.

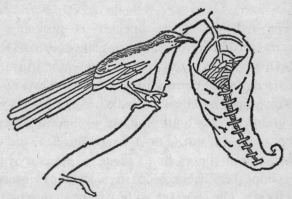

Perhaps the most astonishing kind of nest is built by the tailor-bird of India. Working with his mate, he sews large leaves together to make a container to hold the actual nest. The tailor-birds puncture a series of holes along the edges of a leaf with their sharp beaks. The female stays inside what will be the nest, while the male stays outside. One pushes spider thread or a blade of grass through a hole, the other seizes the thread and pushes it back through the next hole. The thread is then pulled tight and fastened. In this way tailor-birds sew up the outside of their home. When all the work is done they fly round to 'inspect' it, adding extra stitches wherever they may be needed.

Each year many thousands of millions of birds fly northward from their warm winter homes below the Equator to their summer homes in the northern parts of the world. Science does not yet know exactly how or why these small creatures fly such enormous distances as regularly as clockwork.

Most of the over 400 different species of birds in Britain and the 700 in North America either come north to nest in the spring, or south to spend the winter with us. They travel an incredible number of miles on very little food. Swallows, for instance, fly every spring from Africa to England or from Brazil and Argentina to Alaska, a distance of over 7,000 miles. The Arctic tern which may make its nest up in the Arctic Circle in the spring may also spend its winters down in the Antarctic – an annual round trip of about 25,000 miles. It can make this long flight over the ocean because it eats fish and can always get its food from the sea.

Migrating birds also travel at incredible heights. Tiny Asiatic warblers regularly cross the 20,000-foot Himalaya mountains to go from India to

Siberia. No wonder bird migration has been called one of the most mysterious phenomena of nature!

It is believed that migrating birds helped early explorers to discover new lands. The first Hawaiians are said to have followed golden plovers on their spring flight from Tahiti to Hawaii. The migrating shining cuckoo is believed to have guided colonists from the Solomon Islands to New Zealand. And according to their history, early Polynesian explorers carried frigates, or man-o'-war birds, with them in their boats. When they got some distance out to sea, they released the frigatebirds, then followed their flight to unknown lands.

Perhaps the best singer among birds is the American mocking-bird. His Latin name is *Mimus polyglottos*, which means 'many-tongued mimic'. And that is just what he is. Although his own song is the only American bird song that closely resembles the beautiful nightingale's, the mocker can imitate from eighty to a hundred different bird songs and calls. He can also imitate other sounds which he hears, sometimes so clearly as to deceive people. He has been heard whoo-whooing like a locomotive, squeaking like a pump handle, and whistling like a traffic policeman. One mocker cheerfully sang the theme song of a soap-opera which he heard coming from a radio at the same time every morning!

Like his more famous but less versatile cousin

the nightingale, a mocker likes best to sing in the bright moonlight of a warm night. Ornithologists once made a ninety-minute recording of a mockingbird's programme. He successfully imitated a goldfinch, wood thrush, flicker, chickadee and some thirty other birds, as well as a tree frog – without once repeating a song!

9

A Variety of Facts about a Variety of Things

ALMOST anything except the universe can be represented in a model drawn to exact scale. Scientific models show the composition of an atom by using parts that are much larger than the parts of an atom really are. Relief maps show the geography of a country with toy hills, plains and rivers that are much smaller than hills, plains and rivers are in reality. But there simply is not enough room in the whole world in which to place even the smallest scale model of the universe. For if you represented the earth with a grain of sand, you would have to place Alpha Centauri, the star that is nearest to the solar system, about 2,500 miles away.

The largest shadow anyone can see is the shadow the earth casts on the moon during its eclipse.

The lowest temperature in the world was recorded not at the North or South Poles but in northern Siberia. In 1892 the thermometer recorded 90 degrees below zero Fahrenheit. The mercury froze solid and it was impossible to light a match.

The highest temperatures in the world are found in the various deserts, where 120 degrees Fahrenheit in the shade is often reached. Near Tripoli, a record of 136 degrees Fahrenheit in the shade was once reported. And it was much warmer in the sun!

Mount Everest in the Himalaya mountains is scientifically recorded to be the highest peak in the world – but Chimborazo, in the Andes mountains of Ecuador, is actually higher. The reason that Mount Everest holds the record is that mountain heights are measured from the level of the sea. The sea level round Ecuador is farther above the centre of the earth than the sea level near the Himalayas. Therefore, when measured from the closest sea level, Mount Everest 29,002 feet, is higher than Chimborazo, 20,577 feet. If each peak were measured straight up from the centre of the earth, however, Chimborazo would be the higher mountain.

The biggest clams in the world are found in

Indonesia. They grow nearly five feet long, and their shells may weigh up to 500 pounds. These monsters live entirely on seaweed and tiny sea organisms. They do not attack men or animals. But should a person or animal accidentally catch his foot in the space between shells when the clam is open, the shells would immediately snap shut. If this happens in deep water (as has sometimes happened to native divers), the man is held under water so long that he drowns. If it happened on a beach at low tide, the clam could trap the man there until the tide came in and he was then drowned. That is why these huge creatures are nicknamed 'man-eating clams', although they do not eat human beings.

The smallest frog is a Cuban tree-frog which is only three-quarters of an inch long. The largest frog is found in Africa: a ten-inch-long body with twelve-inch-long hind legs.

The fastest-moving creature in the world is the deer botfly. One expert claims to have clocked a deer botfly's speed at 818 miles per hour and to have checked this with a high-speed camera. He says such terrific flying speed is possible because the insects fly at very high altitudes where the wind resistance is less than at ordinary altitudes. At such a rate of speed, and if he had enough endurance, a deer botfly could fly westward round the world in daylight, moving with the sunshine.

Another expert believes 818 miles per hour is an inaccurate estimate. He thinks the deer botfly moves 'only' at the speed of 400 miles per hour. Even at this slower speed, the deer botfly is still the fastest-moving thing.

A bird's feather is considered to be the strongest thing in nature for its size and weight.

Hydrogen is the lightest substance known to science. Osmium, a rare, platinum-like metal, is the heaviest. Osmium weighs 250,000 times as much as hydrogen.

Sound travels at the rate of about 1,000 feet per second through air. But sound will travel nearly five times as fast – close to 5,000 feet per second – through cold water, and fifteen times as fast through iron and steel.

Science is finding new ways of using the energy of supersonic waves. These vibrate from 20,000 to 1,000,000 times per second. They cannot be heard by human ears. But they can be used to kill germs, homogenize milk, eliminate fog, and as depth-finders on ships. Doctors expect that these high-frequency waves may also be used soon to kill certain tumours in the human body, as they have already done in experimental animals.

Even the sound-waves which we can hear may have unusual effects. The bells of Notre Dame Cathedral in Paris are famous for their beautiful tones, but the sound waves they produce are powerful. Many tourists climb the towers and stand near the bells while they are ringing. If they stand too close, they may have a sudden and unexpected nosebleed. The bells' sound waves can rupture the thin blood vessels of the nose.

Man is not a very large animal, but his body statistics include many large numbers and many fascinating facts. For instance:

A baby eats an amount of food equal to his

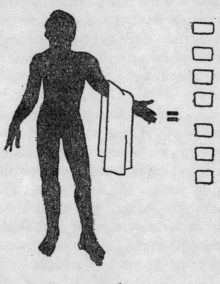

weight every ten days; an adult consumes his own weight in food once every fifty days.

The body of an average-size, full-grown human male contains enough fat to make at least seven cakes of soap, enough phosphorus to make 2,000 match-heads, enough carbon to make 8,500 pencils, enough iron to make one nail, and enough water to fill a 12-gallon barrel.

There are some 12,000,000,000 cells in the human brain.

There are 300,000,000 air cells in both human lungs.

The kidneys have about 280 miles of tiny tubes.

The blood vessels have a combined length of 100,000 miles.

Ten million red blood cells in an adult are destroyed and replaced every second.

There are approximately twenty-five billion (25,000,000,000,000) red blood cells in the average adult human body.

And the average human heart beats 100,800 times a day (almost 40,000,000 times in a single year), pumps 1,500 quarts of blood a day (or almost enough to fill a goods train wagon), and uses enough energy in two hours to lift nearly 60 tons one foot up into the air.

The very smallest speck of dust that a man can see with the naked eye contains approximately one thousand billion atoms.

All atoms are made up of three kinds of electrical particles: protons, neutrons and electrons. This is an example of how infinitely tiny electrons are: if you could increase the size of an electron fifty million times it would still be invisible to the naked eye!

In order to study bacteria or germs, scientists today have a kit full of tools the working parts of which are almost too small to be seen by the naked eye. Such needles, knives, forks and hammers must be used with the help of a microscope. They are called micro-tools. The working end of one of these tiny glass tools may measure only one two-hundred-and-fifty-thousandth of an inch in diameter.

Another valuable scientific instrument is a very delicate scale called the microbalance. Here is the kind of small object this scale can weigh. A sheet of blank paper is first weighed on the microbalance and its weight is noted. The paper is taken off the scale, and with a sharp pencil the experimenter makes one dot on it. When the paper is weighed again, the microbalance shows that the pencil dot weighs ten gammas. (A gamma is one-millionth of a gram.)

The Swiss Government gave the Queen what is believed to be the smallest watch in the world when she was married.

What is probably the longest name given to any place belongs to a small village in Anglesey. Its Welsh name consists of 58 letters: Llanfairpwllgwyngyllgogerychwyrndrobwllllantysiliogogogoch!

The English meaning of this name is 'Mary Church of the Pool of White Hazels rather near the Swift Whirlpool of the Church of Tysilio of the Red Cave'. But it is usually called Llanfair P.G. for short!

10
The Real Facts Are . . .

MANY things which many people repeat from habit are not based on scientific fact. For instance, almost everyone has heard the saying, 'Alike as two peas in a pod'. *The real fact* is that no two peas in a pod are exactly alike. No two snowflakes, no two leaves, no two things made by man or machine, no two things in the whole wide world are *exactly* alike. Scientists even believe that each atom is slightly different from each other atom.

Here are some other popular sayings that are not based on fact:

Slow as a tortoise. *The real fact is* that the tortoise is most at home in the tropics and the heat of a desert. When he lives in a colder climate, he moves more slowly than he does in the warm climate where he can move quite fast for his size and weight.

Wise as an owl. *The real fact is* that although an owl looks wise, he is really slow-witted and rather stupid compared with other birds. Besides, he cannot see in the dark, as many people believe.

Quiet as a mouse. *The real fact is* that mice are not always quiet. When undisturbed in a barn or attic they often play with nuts or other small objects by rolling them on the floor, just to hear the noise they make.

Mad as a hornet. *The real fact is* that a hornet has such a good temper that she seldom loses it. She will sting and attack only when frightened or teased, or when her nest seems to be in danger.

The names of things are often misleading also. For example:

A pineapple is neither an apple nor a pine. It is a kind of berry.

Arabic numerals were first used by Hindus, not by Arabs.

Buttermilk has no butter in it because it is milk from which all the butterfat has been removed.

Banana oil is a by-product of coal, not of a banana, although it has a fruity odour.

The funny bone is not a bone in your elbow but a nerve.

Silverfish are insects.

White ants are rarely white, and they are not ants, but termites.

A lead pencil contains no lead. Its point is made of a form of carbon called graphite.

A ring round the moon at night does not necessarily mean that there will be bad weather the next day. *The real fact is* that these rings, called lunar circles, can and do precede good weather as often as bad.

When you hold a large seashell to your ear, you may hear a rather loud roaring. But this is not the sound of ocean waves, as many people believe. *The real fact is* that some of the sounds that are being made outside the thin shell make the air inside it vibrate. Because of its hollow shape and the smoothness of its inner surface, the shell becomes a 'resonator' of noises around it. So the sounds in the room, as well as the sound of your own pulses in your head, are blended into a roar or rumble. These are the 'ocean waves'.

Steel is often called the most useful metal in the world. *The real fact is* that iron should get the credit for the greatest usefulness, however, because steel is made from iron.

The expression 'seeing red' comes from the idea that bulls become furious at the sight of that colour. *The real fact is* that all cattle are almost totally colour-blind, hence a bull cannot distinguish red from any other colour. What does enrage him is the sight of a bright object waving at a rapid speed. Any quick-moving, light-coloured rag or flag will make a bull angry.

Bears are commonly believed to hug people to death. *The real fact is* that bears stand up on their hind legs when they are alarmed or when they wish to attack. They use their front legs for boxing and clawing, but there is no record of their ever having embraced a person with their front legs and hugged him to death.

Elephants are not afraid of mice.

Many a boy or girl who owns a pet rabbit believes that the best way to lift him is by his long ears. *The real fact is* that this is a very cruel thing to do. A rabbit's ears are extremely sensitive; he can actually be injured if he is lifted by them. The best  way to pick up a rabbit is to grasp the loose skin above his shoulders with one hand, and support his body with the other hand.

Because of their great appetite, goats have been

accused of eating tin cans. *The real fact is* that this is physically impossible. Goats can be seen on rubbish dumps licking at cans in order to lick off the paper labels. The salt in the paper and the glue that makes the labels stick to the tin taste good to goats. They will nibble curiously at almost anything, but they will not, do not and cannot eat shoes, clothing or tins.

Many a story has been told of the clever beaver who fells a tree so that it will fall just exactly where he wants it across a stream. *The real fact is* that a beaver starts gnawing to make the deepest cut in a tree on the side which he can reach the most easily. He then lets the tree fall where it will. Many beavers have been killed by trees which they themselves have felled.

The cartoon of an ostrich hiding his head in the sand has long been used as the perfect example of stupidity in the face of danger. *The real fact is* that ostriches recognize a threat to their safety and depend upon their long legs and great speed to save them. The idea that they bury their heads in the sand probably originated when desert travellers long ago saw ostriches feeding at a distance. An ostrich will poke his beak into holes to look for water, which he often finds under the sand. He also has to bend his head down to the earth in order to eat.

Bats are supposed to fly into your hair if you do not cover your head. This idea probably comes from the idea that bats are blind. And since they usually fly at night, it seems logical to assume that they cannot see where they are going and will become entangled in your hair. But although bats do not see well in the dark, *the real fact is* that they avoid flying into obstacles by means of a sort of radar. They make tiny, shrill squeaks, so high-pitched that humans cannot hear them. The sound waves from these squeaks hit an object and bounce back to a bat's ears in the form of echoes. These echoes prevent a bat from flying into anything in his path.

Clothes moths are blamed for eating our winter clothing in warm weather. *The real fact is* that a full-grown clothes moth does not eat anything. The damage done to woollens and furs is done entirely by the larvae, or wormlike baby moths, that hatch from the eggs a clothes moth lays during its short life.

The large spider known as the tarantula is generally believed to be very poisonous and dangerous to man. *The real fact is* that the bite of this spider is far from lethal and is no more serious than a wasp or bee sting. The tarantula takes its name from Taranto, a town in Italy, near where it is frequently found.

There are probably more myths about snakes than about any other form of animal life. Here are a few incorrect beliefs about snakes, with the *real facts:*

False: Snakes sting with their tongues. *True:* They use their tongues to help them find their way about. Poisonous snakes bite with their fangs, not their tongues.

False: Snakes are slimy. *True:* Snakes have very clean and dry skins.

False: A snake killed during the day will not die until after the sun sets. *True:* A snake dies as soon as it is killed, but its muscles may continue to move for some time after it is dead.

False: A hoop snake can take its tail in its mouth and roll downhill like a hoop. *True:* No snake can do this. There is a reptile called the hoop snake, though.

False: Snakes cannot bite unless they can coil before striking. *True:* When there is time, a snake will coil, then strike. But in an emergency a dangerous snake will try to bite from any position.

False: You can always tell the age of a rattle-snake by the number of rattles on his tail. *True:* If this were true, a rattlesnake would have to produce one rattle every year. Instead he may produce more than one a year, since he gets a new rattle every time he sheds his skin, regardless of his birthday. He may also show fewer than one rattle for each year of his life, as rattles often rub or scrape off his tail when he crawls through crevices in rocks.

False: A cobra dances when a snake-charmer plays certain music. *True:* A cobra does not dance and it is doubtful that he even hears the music. What he is doing when he seems to be dancing is to follow the motions made by the snake-charmer's body. In his natural, wild state, he constantly shifts his position in this way in order always to be ready to strike at the best advantage.

False: A rattlesnake always rattles before he strikes. *True:* He may strike without making a sound.

Many housewives believe that if you place a silver spoon in a glass before pouring hot liquid into the glass, the spoon will always prevent the heat from breaking the glass. *The real fact is* that it is risky to count on this. Although the silver spoon does conduct heat, it is doubtful if under all conditions it could conduct enough heat compared with the heat of the liquid to prevent the glass from breaking.

People often think that thunderstorms cause milk to turn sour. *The real fact is* that thunderstorms usually occur towards the end of a hot summer's day. Since refrigeration is not always 100 per cent perfect (and many people may not have any refrigeration at all), the milk probably turned sour before the storm arose. If this fact was not noticed until after the storm had passed, you can see how someone might conclude that the storm, rather than the heat, had soured the milk.

Many cooks keep a high flame under a pot after its contents have started to boil in order to be sure they continue to boil. *The real fact is* that once water bubbles at the boiling point, the flame under it can be turned down low enough just to keep it bubbling. A high flame cannot make the fluid any hotter than it is when it boils. A low flame will save money on the gas bill but still cook food thoroughly.

For centuries there have been myths about food which science has since discovered to be untrue. For instance:
   'Crusts make your hair curl'.
   'Garlic purifies the blood'.

'Meat makes you want to fight'.

These are just a few of the superstitions about food which simply are not true.

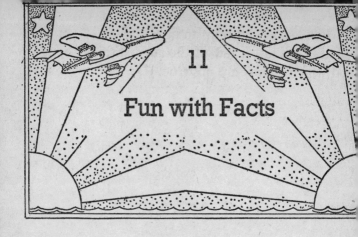

11

Fun with Facts

THE fact that a fact is a fact does not mean it is dull! Quizzes with scientific answers can be entertaining. Tricks to demonstrate scientific truths can be amusing. Here are some questions and some simple home experiments which you may use to amaze your friends while, at the same time, you have fun.

Question: Is there any place in the Western Hemisphere where the sun rises in the Pacific Ocean?

Answer: Yes. In certain parts of the Isthmus of Panama, the sun rises in the Pacific and sets in the Atlantic. This is because the Isthmus curves in such a way that the end farthest to the east touches the Pacific Ocean, while the end farthest to the west touches the Atlantic.

Question: If you were to stand directly on top of the site of the North Pole, facing south, what direction would be on your left? On your right?

Answer: South would be the only direction to your left and right and all round you.

Question: How much do you think a cube of solid gold measuring fourteen inches on all sides would weigh? Five pounds? Five hundred pounds? One ton?

Answer: About one ton.

Question: There are at least eight metals that are more valuable than gold. Can you name them?

Answer: Radium, platinum, osmium, iridium, rhodium, ruthenium, cerium, uranium.

Question: Twelve metals are heavier than lead. Can you name them?

Answer: Gold, osmium, mercury, platinum, tungsten, uranium, iridium, palladium, rhodium, ruthenium, tantalum, thallium.

Question: Suppose a plane could fly from New York to Los Angeles at a steady 1,000 miles per hour, without stopping. This distance is 3,500 miles, so the flight would take three and a half hours. If the plane left New York at noon, it would arrive in Los Angeles at 11.30 a.m. How is this possible?

Answer: The plane is moving towards the west faster than the earth is turning towards the east. This means the plane would continually fly faster than the sunlight as it reaches the earth. So the plane actually reaches the west half an hour before the time it left the east, although it flew through the air for three and a half hours.

Question: Almost everyone has been tricked by the old question, 'Which is the heavier, a pound of feathers or a pound of gold?' Do *you* know the right answer?

Answer: If the pound of feathers and the pound of gold were both weighed by the same system of weights, they would both weigh the same. But technically, the pound of feathers weighs more than the pound of gold for this reason: feathers are usually weighed by avoirdupois weight, which equals 7,000 grains to a pound. Gold, on the other hand, is usually weighed by troy weight which only equals 5,760 grains to a pound.

Question: Which weighs more, a cubic foot of warm water, or a cubic foot of cold water?

Answer: The cold water weighs more because it has more molecules in it than warm water. One cubic foot of warm water weighs 61·998 pounds while one cubic foot of cold water weighs 62·416 pounds. Water is heaviest at a temperature of four degrees Centigrade.

Question: Which weighs more, a quart of double cream or a quart of single cream?

Answer: A quart of single cream weighs more than a quart of double cream because double cream contains more fat. This fat weighs less than its equivalent amount of liquid in the single cream. For this reason, cream rises to the top of a bottle of milk.

Question: Can a moving object ever change the direction in which it is moving without first stopping, then going off in the new direction?

Answer: No. Even a bullet that is fired straight up into the sky has to stop an instant at the top of its journey before it changes direction and descends to earth.

Question: Does snow melt faster in the country or in town?

Answer: Snow usually melts faster in town because there it quickly becomes covered with a fine coat of soot or dust. A dark or dirty surface absorbs heat from the sun while a clean, bright surface reflects the sun's rays and so remains cool for a longer time. That is why clean snow in the countryside melts more slowly than soiled snow in the town.

Question: If a rubber ball, a steel ball and a wooden ball of the same size are thrown with equal force on a pavement, which do you think will bounce the highest into the air?

Answer: The steel ball will bounce the highest, then the rubber one and lastly, the wooden one. This is because steel can be more quickly compressed and will more quickly return to its original shape than rubber. This compression (when the

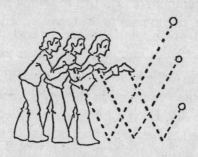

ball hits the pavement) and return to shape (which forces the ball up into the air) is what determines how high a ball will bounce. Rubber compresses easily, but it is comparatively slow in returning to its original size.

Question: Cement and concrete are the same materials with two different names. True or false?

Answer: False. Cement is one of the ingredients of concrete. Concrete is made of a mixture of sand or gravel with water. It is hardened by cement which is used to bind the materials together.

Question: Shellac is obtained from pine trees, sea water, a scale insect, or coal tar?

Answer: A scale insect.

Question: A spider is an insect with eight legs. True or false?

Answer: False. A spider is not an insect.

Question: How many hairs are there on the average human head? 20,000 to 50,000? 50,000 to 75,000? 100,000 to 150,000?

Answer: The actual number depends upon the coarseness of the hair, but 100,000 is average. A red-headed woman may have 90,000 while a blonde with very fine hair may have as many as 140,000.

Question: What animal looks like a piece of rock?

Answer: Coral.

A WHICH-IS-WHAT, TRUE-OR-FALSE QUIZ

1. A ladybird is a beautiful female bird. True or false? *Answer:* False. A ladybird is a kind of beetle.

2. A mud puppy is a kind of mud-loving little dog. True or false? *Answer:* False. A mud puppy is a large aquatic salamander.

3. A laughing jackass is a kind of bird. True or false? *Answer:* True.

4. A sea elephant is an elephant that can swim. True or false? *Answer:* False. A sea elephant is a kind of seal.

5. A flying fox is a large tropical bat. True or false? *Answer:* True.

6. A ship-worm is a worm that is often found on ships. True or false? *Answer:* False. A ship-worm is a kind of shellfish that burrows into wooden ships.

Question: What animal can be used in your bath? *Answer:* A sponge.

Question: Which animals get up with their hind legs first when they have been lying down? *Answer:* Cattle, sheep, goats, antelope, deer, giraffes, and all members of the cud-chewing family rise with their hind legs first. All other four-footed animals use their front legs first.

Here's a question with which you may have some fun, especially with your father. Sir Walter Raleigh did much to make smoking popular: he once bet some friends of his that he could calculate exactly how much smoke there was in a pound of tobacco. He won his bet by doing something very simple. What did he do?

Answer: He smoked a pound of tobacco, carefully saving all the ashes. Then he weighed the ashes and subtracted their weight from one pound.

The difference between the weight of the ashes and one pound gave him the answer as to how much smoke there was in the pound of tobacco.

Question: Can an expert tell, by looking at a drop of blood through a microscope, whether that blood came from a Negro, a white man, an Indian or a Chinese?

Answer: No. All human beings belong to the zoological species called *Homo sapiens*, and their blood is the same.

Enough of questions. Let's try some easy experiments which you can do at home.

Do you want to amaze your friends and family? Ask them how they would make sheets of paper stick to a very smooth wall without using any kind of glue, paste or rubber cement, nor any tacks, nails or pins. When they give up, simply rub the papers briskly with your hand or the back of a comb for a minute or two. Then clap the papers on

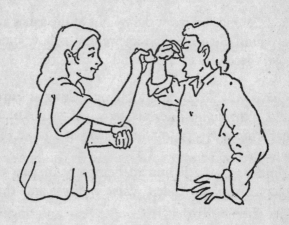

he wall. The static electricity will keep the papers ticking to the smooth surface.

Your senses of touch and taste may usually be relied upon to tell you the truth. But not always. Try this on yourself, then on your friends. Close your eyes tight and hold your nose. Then ask someone to give you a bite of raw apple or a bite of raw potato without telling you which is which. You will not be able to tell whether you are tasting apple or a potato.

Here is another taste-deceiver. Take a clean, unpainted stick of wood. Open your mouth and very carefully put the end of the wood on the back part of your tongue. The wood will taste bitter.

Now take the very same stick and put its end on the tip of your tongue. The wood will taste sweet. At the sides of your tongue it will taste sour.

The wood really has no taste at all. But it tastes bitter or sweet or sour according to the taste buds on your tongue.

Nor can you always believe what you feel with your fingers. To prove this fact, try the following. Take a marble and hold it between your crossed first and second fingers, as you see in the picture. Now close your eyes and roll the marble about on a table top, holding it always between your two crossed fingers so that it touches first one finger, then the other. Since you know there is only one marble, you would naturally expect to feel only one. But your sense of touch distinctly feels two marbles.

This odd fact was known to scientists more than two thousand years ago, but the reason for it is still

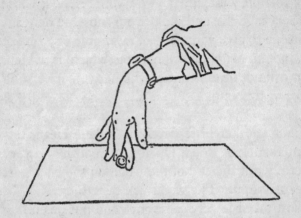

not certain. It is believed that the unfamiliar sensation is interpreted incorrectly by the brain.

Here's an interesting demonstration of how air pressure works. Take a flat hard-rubber sink plug, the kind that has a ring in its centre. Wet the bottom of the plug and place it on the seat of a flat-topped stool. Make sure there is no air between the seat and the plug. Now tie a string through the plug's ring. With the help of no other force except the pressure of the outside air upon the top of the sink plug, you can then lift up the stool by the string

Did you know that although zinc gauze is much heavier than water, it can be made to float? To prove this, fill a bowl with water. Take a small square of gauze and carefully lay it flat on the surface of the water. It will not only float there, but it will support the weight of a cork if you place the cork gently in the middle of the piece of gauze.

But in order to make this 'raft' sink all you have to do is to dip a corner of a bar of soap in the bowl of water, without touching the gauze.

The reason the zinc floats in the first place is because the surface of the water 'stretches' like a very thin elastic. Light, flat, waterproof articles can float on this elastic surface without breaking through it.

But certain substances, such as soap, lower this 'surface tension' as it is called. So when you touch a bit of soap to the water, the gauze sinks.

Speaking of soap, would you like to make a little model boat which will move across water without any sails or engine?

PUT SOAP HERE

Cut a piece of cardboard in the shape of a boat with a pointed front and a square back. Make a small V-shaped cut in the square back, and place a tiny bit of soap in this V.

Now fill a bowl with water, and place your soap-powered boat on the water's surface. The boat will immediately begin to move all over the water in the basin until the surface tension is entirely weakened by the soap.

The secret behind this mystery motor lies in the bit of soap. As it dissolves, the soap weakens the surface tension of the water directly behind the boat. The tension directly ahead of it is stronger, so the boat is pulled forward on to the firmer 'skin' of water. This continues until the soap has weakened the surface of all the water in the basin.

While you're in the kitchen, suppose you take a raw egg and a hard-boiled egg from the refrigerator. Do you know how to tell which is which?

Place each egg on a saucer. Now briskly spin the eggs, watching what each one does. The egg that is hard-boiled will spin steadily for quite a while. The raw egg will spin slowly, wobble around, then soon stop.

The reason for this behaviour on the part of the raw egg is that it is filled with a semi-liquid, while the hard-boiled egg is solid. For complex physical reasons a solid substance tends to retain motion longer than a liquid substance does.

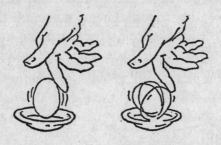

There is nothing useful about a glass full of dancing mothballs, unless your father happens to own a shop and would like to place such an attraction in its window. But here is a simple experiment which is fun to do and to watch.

Fill a tall glass or transparent vase with water. Add one tablespoonful of white vinegar and stir. Then slowly add one half-teaspoonful of bicarbonate of soda. The mixture will immediately fizz. While it is still bubbling, drop five or six mothballs into the glass. Within a few minutes, one ball after the other will slowly rise to the top of the water, stay there a second, then drop to the bottom. And they will repeat this fascinating 'perpetual motion' every few minutes for several hours.

What is the 'motor' that makes the mothballs

move? Look at them closely. You will see that bubbles of carbon dioxide, made by the reaction of the vinegar to the bicarbonate of soda, cling to the outside of the mothballs. Whenever these bubbles become large enough, they float the mothball to the surface of the water. There, some of the gas bubbles get knocked off, and down the mothball sinks – only to accumulate more gas bubbles and rise and sink again and again.

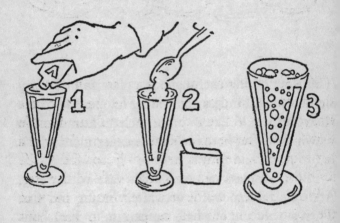

The next time you have some guests for dinner ask them this.

Here is an ice-cube floating in a cup of water. And here is a short length of string. Using only the items usually found on a dinner table, without tying the string round the ice or using a spoon, can you remove the ice cube from the water?

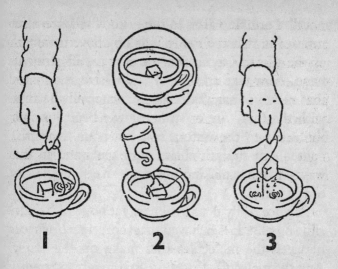

I	**2**	**3**

If your guests say no, this is the way you can show them how to do the trick. Wet the end of the string and lay it across the ice cube. Then sprinkle a little salt along each side of the string. Within a few moments, the string becomes frozen fast to the ice cube, and you can easily lift it out of the cup.

Why? Because salt lowers the freezing point of the ice which it touches, causing it to melt. But when it melts, the salted ice steals heat from the rest of the ice and from the water on the string. And as the heat is stolen from them, they freeze together.

And let's end these experiments with a real scientific mystery – an amazing trick for which there is as yet no completely accurate answer.

Fill a drinking glass to the brim with water, but not so full that the top rounds up above the edges of the glass. Keep a thin wire or a stiff straw at hand. Now take an ordinary table-size salt shaker that is full of salt. Stirring the water all the time with the thin wire or straw, slowly begin to pour the salt into the water. You can pour the entire contents of the salt shaker into the water in this way – without making the water overflow the rim of the glass!

Science really does not know yet how this is possible or why. It is believed that there may be spaces between the molecules that make up the water. And the molecules that make up the salt apparently can fit into these spaces without adding to the total volume. Perhaps this is a mystery you may help to solve some day.

If you have enjoyed this
PICCOLO Book you may like
to choose your next book from
the titles listed on the following pages.

Piccolo Non-Fiction

Jean Stroud
PICCOLO ENCYCLOPEDIA OF
USEFUL FACTS (illus)   30p

Here's the new, revised edition of a Piccolo
favourite, with bang-up-to-date facts about
Sport, Space, History, Money, Nature, Pop
Music – and hundreds of other things.
Whether it's for learning or simply for fun,
you'll find this a treasure trove of fascinating
information – clear, quick and easy to use.

Piccolo TV/Times

HOW (illus)   20p
A SECOND BOOK OF HOW (illus) 25p

If it's not just facts you're after, and you want
to know just HOW things are made, HOW
things work, HOW things came about, then
these General Knowledge Question and
Answer Books are a must! They're based
on the highly popular Southern TV series, and
they've got all the answers to a wide range of
intriguing questions – anything from the origin
of April Fool's Day to the way Stonehenge
was built.

Piccolo Puzzles and Games

David Webster
BRAIN BOOSTERS (illus)   20p

Here are 300 Science Riddles, Puzzles and
Brainteasers – an intriguing voyage of discovery for the curious of all ages! Meet the
Bleeps and the Fubbyloofers ... learn how to
make balloon-rockets and identify fingerprints ... experiment with thermometers and
wham-wham jars ... Each section has something for everyone – entertaining, informative
and definitely Brain Boosting!

John Jaworski and Ian Stewart
NUT-CRACKERS (illus)   20p

Puzzles and games to boggle the mind! You'll
find all sorts of things to do, things to make
and things to look at in this entertaining book –
word games, code games, string puzzles, mazes,
number patterns, skeleton crosswords – and
not forgetting of course Professor Crank-
shaft's Impossible Objects!

Piccolo Puzzles and Games

Captain Ralph S. Barnaby
HOW TO MAKE AND FLY
PAPER AIRCRAFT   25p

Through the simple instructions and clear
illustrations of this book, you can learn not
only how to build paper gliders both basic and
more sophisticated – you'll also develop an
understanding of the fundamental principles
of flight and flight control. All you need is
paper, sticky tape, scissors and paper clips, and
you're ready to follow the flight path of the
Wright brothers!

Norvin Pallas
CODE GAMES (illus)   20p

From the ciphers of Sherlock Holmes to secret
Naval Intelligence ciphers, here are hundreds
of intriguing and puzzling games. So now you
too can send secret messages ... use trick
passwords and keywords ... and soon you'll
be inventing your own to baffle and amuse
your family and friends.